THE
INTERNET
AND
THE
FIRST
AMENDMENT

Schools and Sexually Explicit Expression

FRED H. CATE

Phi Delta Kappa Educational Foundation
Bloomington, Indiana
U.S.A.

Cover design by
Victoria Voelker

Cover illustration by
Christopher Ganz

Phi Delta Kappa Educational Foundation
408 North Union Street
Post Office Box 789
Bloomington, Indiana 47402-0789
U.S.A.

Printed in the United States of America

Library of Congress Catalog Card Number 97-75653
ISBN 0-87367-398-0

ACKNOWLEDGMENTS

I have benefited greatly from my colleagues at Indiana University, Ice Miller Donadio & Ryan, and the Annenberg Washington Program in Communications Policy Studies, as well as from the many opportunities afforded me by the Indiana Library Federation to develop and refine ideas in the company of experienced and thoughtful professionals. These individuals and institutions will, of course, not agree with all of my conclusions; but they have been nonetheless influential in helping me form them.

I also am fortunate to work with two excellent research assistants — April Sellers and Molly Moran — and two patient and talented secretaries — Mary Michelle Yager and Marjorie Young.

I appreciate the opportunity provided by Phi Delta Kappa to write this volume, and I particularly thank Donovan R. Walling, editor of Phi Delta Kappa's Special Publications, for making this project possible.

Finally, I am grateful to my wife, Beth, who provides me with endless support, while challenging my ideas, logic, assumptions, writing, and even my punctuation. No author could ask for anything more.

TABLE OF CONTENTS

INTRODUCTION

Computers and the networks that connect them have rapidly become a dominant force in business, government, education, entertainment, and virtually all other aspects of society in the United States and throughout the world. The International Telecommunication Union predicts that by the turn of the century information services and products — already the world's largest economic sector — will account for $3.5 trillion in revenue.

Nowhere is the remarkable prominence and power of electronic information clearer than in the case of the Internet — the most ubiquitous of information networks. The Internet links more than 60 million users in 190 countries. These users connect to each other and to a dazzling array of online services and products with staggering speed and frequency. As of July 1997 there were more than 19.5 million World Wide Web hosts; one year earlier there were fewer than 13 million hosts; in 1993, there were fewer than two million. The growth in commercial online services — the bellwether of future financial stability for the Internet — is equally dramatic. In July 1997 more than 4.5 million Internet hosts were designated ".com" for commercial. One year earlier, only 3.3 million of those companies were present on the Internet. In 1994, only one million hosts were designated ".com."[1] These figures tend to underestimate the size of the Internet, but they provide a reliable benchmark as to its dramatic growth.

Educators and politicians have not been slow to recognize the potential of the Internet for education at all levels. Instantaneous, low-cost access to text, images, and sounds from around the world; the potential for individualized, self-directed exploration; and the practical ability to link numerous, distant sites, whether all of the schools in a district or state or all of the teachers and

1

students interested in a specific topic from around the nation — all have dazzled many government officials, school administrators, teachers, and librarians.

During the run-up to the 1992 presidential election, Bill Clinton and Al Gore campaigned on a promise to create a network that would "link every home, business, lab, classroom and library by the year 2015."[2] President Clinton made the same promise in his first inaugural address, and his Administration subsequently established a matching grant program, administered by the National Telecommunications and Information Administration, that during the President's first term provided almost $12 million in federal seed money for Internet-related projects in K-12 schools and more than $4.5 million toward similar projects in libraries.

By 1996 the World Wide Web's point-and-click graphic interface had made the Internet easier to use, more resources were being made available via Internet, and government officials' interest in information technologies in schools and libraries was rising. In the Telecommunications Act of 1996, Congress specified that "[e]lementary and secondary schools and classrooms . . . and libraries should have access to advanced telecommunication services," and directed the Federal Communications Commission to tax telecommunications service providers to subsidize the cost of that access.[3] In May 1997 the commission adopted a plan requiring telecommunications service providers to provide 20% to 90% discounts to schools and libraries for accessing information technology services, thereby subsidizing that access by $2.25 billion every year.[4]

In their bid for a second term, President Clinton and Vice President Gore advanced the target date of their pledge, from 2015 to 2000, to wire every American classroom and library. In the first State of the Union address of his second term, the President proposed three goals for the nation's public education system. One of the three was that "every 12-year-old must be able to log on to the Internet."[5] The President also reiterated his plan "to connect every classroom and library to the Internet by the year 2000."[6]

Just days after the inauguration, the President announced $200 million in federal grants, administered by the Department of Education, to provide schools with computers and Internet training. The President also sent to Congress a 1998 budget proposing $500 million annually for "technology literacy" grants for four years — a $2 billion grant program. He then set out on a New Deal-style education campaign, based on a 10-point challenge, including "[c]onnect every classroom and library to the Internet by 2000."[7]

Telecommunications service providers, responding to such political pressure, hoping to forestall further regulation, and seeking to build customer loyalty, also have jumped on the bandwagon. In October 1995 AT&T pledged $150 million over five years to connect schools to the Internet. In July 1996 the cable television industry offered to provide elementary and secondary schools free high-speed equipment for linking to the Internet. Service providers also are participating in "NetDays," modern-day barn raisings, inaugurated by President Clinton in California in 1996, in which private companies and community volunteers are helping to lay the cable and fiber infrastructure necessary for connecting schools to the Internet.

While educators, politicians, and service providers herald the potential of the Internet in classrooms and libraries, many questions are being raised about the financial cost of access and the necessary computers and software; the priority being placed on Internet access as opposed to buildings, teachers, and textbooks; the value of Internet in elementary and secondary education; and the need for training teachers and librarians in the use of rapidly changing technologies.

These difficult questions are exacerbated by the power and complexity of the Internet itself. The Internet is extraordinarily diverse. It is composed of millions of computers, networks, data files, and services. These encompass a tremendous variety of information. The Internet is inherently global. It is unique among information media in crossing not only every state boundary, but also most national borders. The Internet also crosses the regulatory boundaries that define U.S. law. The technologies of the Internet, which are many and complex in their own right, play havoc with many cultural and legal assumptions about how information is created, delivered, and accessed; who should be responsible for its stewardship and use; under what conditions it should be available to the public; and who should be liable when information causes harm.

Among the important issues posed by the rush to wire classrooms and libraries to the Internet are those concerning what children may find on the Internet and the responsibility and liability of teachers, librarians, and administrators for controlling, or failing to control, access to that content. This book examines one of the most significant of these content-related questions: the laws governing children's access to sexually explicit expression. The book focuses on expression through the Internet, because that is the most common means through which sexually explicit expression is accessible in American schools and libraries and because that is the context in which much of the current controversy over such expression arises. However, the discussion is applicable to expression by means of other media.

The goals of this volume are three-fold: 1) to provide teachers and librarians with a clear, understandable framework of the legal issues presented by minors' access to sexually explicit material; 2) to offer practical information about the advisability and practicality of attempting to control that access; and 3) to identify important issues for professional and classroom discussion concerning the regulation of such access. This volume will not substitute for legal advice addressing a specific situation involving sexually explicit expression in the classroom, but it will help clarify when legal advice may be needed and help make the advice more useful. Moreover, this volume does not address the complex interaction among teachers, librarians, administrators, school boards, and parents in the educational arena. As a practical matter, how much access to Internet content a specific student is permitted is likely to be the result of a subtle mix of school policies and resources, parental preferences, and teacher or librarian oversight.

The law may be largely irrelevant. More important, even if protected by the law, an individual teacher or librarian may suffer serious consequences if he or she ignores institutional policies, administrative directives, or parental wishes. The interaction among education decision-makers is a significant issue, but it has been well addressed elsewhere and is beyond the scope of this book.

Rather than focus on *who* makes the determination about students' access to sexually explicit expression, this volume examines the legal issues affecting *whether* to permit that access and *how much* access to allow. In sum, this book is intended to facilitate meaningful discussion about the regulation of minors' access to sexually explicit material and the role of educational institutions and individual teachers and librarians in controlling such access.

Notes

1. Network Wizards' semi-annual Internet Domain Surveys are available at http://nw.com/.
2. Bill Clinton, "A National Economic Strategy for America," 21 June 1992. (Available through U.S. Newswire, 19 June 1992).
3. Telecommunications Act of 1996, Pub. L. No. 104-104, §§ 101(a), 254(b)(6), 254(e), 110 Stat. 56, 72-73 [to be codified at 47 U.S.C. §§ 254(b)(6), 254(e)].
4. First Report and Order (FCC 97-158), CC Docket No. 96-45, 1997 FCC LEXIS 2332 (7 May 1997) (FCC report and order).
5. "President Clinton's Message to Congress on the State of the Union," *New York Times*, 5 February 1997, p. A20.
6. Id.
7. Peter Applebome, "With New Deal Fervor, Clinton Pushes Education Plan," *New York Times*, 6 February 1997, p. B8.

CHAPTER ONE

THE INTERNET AND SEXUALLY EXPLICIT EXPRESSION

The Internet began in 1969 as an experimental project of the U.S. Defense Department's Advanced Research Project Agency (ARPA). Originally called ARPANET, the network linked computers and computer networks owned by the military, defense contractors, and universities conducting defense-related research. The network was later expanded to allow researchers around the country access to powerful supercomputers located at key universities and research laboratories.[1]

From its inception, the network was designed to be a decentralized, self-maintaining series of redundant links among computers, capable of rapidly transmitting communications and rerouting them automatically if one or more individual links were damaged or otherwise unavailable. The goal was to allow defense research and communications to continue even if portions of the network were damaged by nuclear blast. To achieve this resilience, ARPANET both encouraged the creation of multiple links among the computers on the network and allowed messages to be broken down into separate "packets," each of which carried the address of its destination so that they could be routed separately from sender to receiver. Thus a message might travel over any number of redundant routes to its destination, and different portions of the message might travel over different routes. The choice of route for each "packet" is made automatically at each network intersection.

The Internet evolved from ARPANET as more universities and, later, organizations with no ties to defense research were connected. The Internet is constituted of literally millions of computers and computer networks. Therefore, content comes not from identified content providers, as is the case with television and newspapers, but from all of the computers that also are receivers and processors of information. As a result, the Internet is truly interactive: Every person who is connected is both a supplier and receiver of information. And unlike telephones, which also are interactive, most Internet data can be accessed by anyone who is online, even multiple users at the same time. Creation and control of Internet content, therefore, are in the hands of millions of disparate businesses, education institutions, government agencies, and individuals.

Internet services may be divided generally into three broad categories. Electronic mail (e-mail) allows one user to communicate with another or with a service provider. E-mail also permits users to subscribe to "lists," so that they automatically receive all e-mail messages posted by other subscribers. Like its postal counterpart — "snail mail," as Internet aficionados refer to it — e-mail is used to deliver a growing volume of unsolicited junk mail offering everything from Girl Scout cookies to legal services. Internet users generate approximately 100 million e-mail messages every day, and more than half of all U.S. employers use e-mail to communicate with their employees. In fact, computers deliver more mail each day than does the U.S. Postal Service.[2] Other point-to-point Internet services are evolving rapidly, including digital audio telephone conversations, which use Internet technologies to carry traditional telephone traffic.

The second general category of Internet services is electronic bulletin boards — "newsgroups" in Internet parlance — in which users can post messages for all other bulletin board subscribers to read; and users can read and respond to the messages, images, and video and sound clips posted by all other users. Newsgroups are organized into "hierarchies," each of which begins with a short abbreviation providing some general idea of the nature of the groups included with each hierarchy. For example, "rec.sport. skating.ice.figure" is a newsgroup in the "recreation" hierarchy and includes messages dealing with figure skating. Similarly, "rec.sport.skating.inline" is in the same hierarchy but deals with in-line skating. The major newsgroup hierarchies include:

alt	"alternative" and often controversial topics
bionet	biological research
bit	popular e-mail lists from BitNet
clari	a series of newsgroups from commercial news servers
comp	computers and related subjects
k12	newsgroups devoted to K-12 education curriculum, language exchanges with native speakers, and classroom-to-classroom projects designed by teachers
law	legal issues
misc	material that does not fit elsewhere
rec	"recreation" information, including hobbies, games, sports, and arts
sci	"sciences" other than biology
soc	"social" groups and topics
talk	politics and related topics

There also are hierarchies dedicated to specific organizations and geographic locations. Indiana University, for example, hosts more than 100 newsgroups in the "iu" hierarchy; there are a similar number of "microsoft" groups.

Newsgroups are carried in many locations throughout the Internet, typically on the larger "servers" operated by universities and commercial service providers. However, not all servers carry all newsgroups. This is particularly true for controversial subjects within the "alt" hierarchy and for hierarchies dedicated to specific organizations.

An Internet user can connect most easily to those newsgroups carried on the server that he or she uses to access the Internet. For example, a person who accesses the Internet through America Online will have easiest access to the newsgroups that America Online carries on its server. But it also is possible to connect to newsgroups carried on other servers.

There are more than 150,000 bulletin boards in North America alone; users post approximately 100 million messages every day. New types of these services are developing rapidly, such as "chat rooms," where diverse Internet users communicate with each other in real time, which is much like the textual equivalent of conference calls.

The third group of Internet offerings includes a wide range of online services and products, such as electronic merchandise catalogues, online airline reservations systems, and electronic access to law and library catalogues and to thousands of other searchable databases. While these Internet services are provided by a wide variety of institutions and individuals, this is the area of fastest commercial online growth. These services are provided today primarily through the World Wide Web.

The World Wide Web is a graphic interface that makes all of these services easier to use. The Web allows a user to "click," using a computer mouse, on a highlighted term so that the computer automatically retrieves the site or text or service linked to that term. Cumbersome text-based commands are replaced with a single "click," and processes previously requiring a series of instructions that had to be learned and memorized are now fully automated. Moreover, powerful new Internet browsers, such as Netscape Communicator and Microsoft Internet Explorer, recognize and correctly act on the variety of data and services available through the Internet: Text is displayed as text; images are configured and displayed as images; recorded sounds are played as music or speech; e-mail is sent as e-mail; and files requested for downloading and storage are directed to the user's hard drive. Finally, the growth of the Internet and easy-to-use interfaces has led to the proliferation of effective search engines that allow users to identify and access information or sites on a given subject or associated with a specified institution or individual.

The Internet in Classrooms and Libraries

It is very difficult to obtain accurate, current data on the availability and use of the Internet in classrooms and libraries. The Department of Education reported in the fall of 1996 that 50% of U.S. K-12 *schools* had some form of Internet access, up from 35% in 1994. But only 9% of *classrooms* reportedly had Internet access, up from 3% in 1994. Moreover, "Internet access" is a vague term, which includes as little as a single computer with a dial-up connection to the Internet. State surveys suggest that far fewer than 50% of schools have the computers, software, and the connection capability necessary for meaningful Internet access. For example, a 1996 survey of Massachusetts school districts found that more than half of computers in elementary schools were more than five years old and incapable of running current educational software. Only one-quarter of computers at all school levels were equipped for multimedia, CD-ROMs, or the Internet.[3] According to the U.S. Department of Education, only one in five teachers uses information technologies and only 13% of public schools require that their teachers be trained in those technologies.[4]

Public libraries reflect greater Internet use. However, for the moment, there may be a larger percentage of libraries than schools with no Internet access. The American Library Association reports that in 1996, 45% of public libraries were connected to the Internet, with 70% of the remaining libraries planning to connect within 12 months. However, 94% of libraries serving populations of 100,000 or more — the libraries that serve the majority of the U.S. population — offer Internet access for their staffs; 52% offer such access to the patrons with a staff intermediary; and 49% offer Internet access directly to patrons.[5]

Despite what might appear to be the low number of classrooms and smaller public libraries connected to the Internet, it is clear that the Internet is a growing presence in schools across the country. Only 5% of all U.S. schools report having no plans to obtain Internet access. And the extraordinary subsidy for such access under the Telecommunications Act of 1996 is only adding to the rapid growth in schools' and libraries' Internet access.

Sexually Explicit Expression on the Internet

Despite the extraordinary variety of information available on the Internet, journalists and regulators have focused attention on the sexually explicit expression found there. One of the earliest public controversies about sexual content on the Internet was sparked on 3 November 1994, when Carnegie Mellon University's vice president of computing services, William Arms, circulated a memo notifying "[m]embers of the campus community" that computer bulletin boards "known to be used for the distribution of sexually explicit or obscene material" would be discontinued from the university's computer systems. The memo claimed that Pennsylvania law required the action. Computing services subsequently indicated that it would be removing all newsgroups containing either sexually explicit text or images.

The administration's action was prompted not by a threatened lawsuit but by information on an undergraduate research project by an electrical engineering student, Marty Rimm. Rimm, who was later to publish his controversial study on so-called cybersex in the *Georgetown Law Journal*, claimed that he had downloaded more than 900,000 sexually explicit images from Internet newsgroups accessible through the university's computer system.[6] In fact, many of those images came from computer bulletin board services that users access directly by telephone, rather than through the Internet. Administration officials claimed to fear that, because Rimm had informed them that the images were accessible through the university's computer system, the university might be found liable under Pennsylvania's obscenity law if it failed to remove the newsgroups from which these images reportedly were downloaded. The newsgroups still would be accessible on the university's computers through other computer servers that carried them, but the Carnegie Mellon server would no longer "mount" them.

The university community quickly voiced widespread opposition to these actions. The administration responded by agreeing to remove only those newsgroups containing sexually explicit images, instead of either text or images, and to form a campus committee to review that decision. That committee ultimately adopted a written policy, which provides for removing only those newsgroups whose "stated purpose and content" violates the law or that "consistently violates over a reasonable trial period legal canons regardless of the stated purpose of the newsgroup."[7] Under this policy, the committee recommended the reinstatement of four newsgroups containing images, the continued exclusion of seven newsgroups containing images, and the university's continued provision of all text-based newsgroups, including those containing sexually explicit material.[8] The committee also recommended the creation of a permanent advisory committee to provide advice to the president and provost about future Internet content matters.

While Carnegie Mellon administrators were backing down, the University of Michigan was opening the second highly publicized chapter in the controversy over sexually explicit expression on the Internet. On 2 February 1995 University of Michigan President James Duderstadt summarily suspended an undergraduate, Jake Baker, for posting a sexually explicit story and e-mail messages that used the name of a fellow undergraduate. Baker had posted his story, which described abduction, sexual torture, and murder, to the Internet newsgroup, "alt.sex.stories." University public safety officials met Baker as he walked out of class on February 2, took him to his dorm to pack a few possessions, and then escorted him off campus. Duderstadt justified the action on the basis that Baker's continuing presence on campus constituted a threat to the health and safety of the student body. The president had been moved to act not by any campus outcry over Baker's postings — that came *after* the university made them public — but rather when an alumnus from Moscow called the newsgroup story to his attention.

One week later, Baker was arrested and indicted for allegedly violating 18 U.S.C. § 875(c), which criminalizes the "transmi[ssion] in interstate or foreign commerce [of] any communications containing any threat to kidnap any person or any threat to injure the person of another."[9] The statute provides for a fine or imprisonment for "not more than five years" or both. Baker was denied bail on two separate occasions. One judge, Bernard Friedman, remarked, "I would not want my daughter on the streets of Ann Arbor or Ohio [where Baker's family lived] with a man in the condition I believe he is in now."[10] Baker was confined in Milan Federal Prison until Judge Avern Cohn finally ordered him released on March 9 on $10,000 bond.

A grand jury reindicted Baker on March 15. The new indictment omitted any charges based on the story, but instead focused on an e-mail correspondence Baker had engaged in with Arthur Gonda, a man never identified by authorities. Baker and the unknown Gonda had exchanged more than 40 messages describing plans for abducting, torturing, and killing young girls and women.

On 21 June 1995 Judge Cohn granted Baker's motion to quash the indictment. In his opinion Judge Cohn held that the e-mail messages did not constitute a "true threat," which he defined as "some language construable as a serious expression of an intent imminently to carry out some injurious act." Judge Cohn found that, even when viewed in the light most favorable to the prosecution, "there is no case for a jury because the factual proof is insufficient as a matter of law."[11]

Judge Cohn went on to highlight several concerns about the prosecution. First, he noted that Baker made no effort to communicate the messages to the student named in his story and, in fact, included a warning to unsuspecting readers that "[t]he following story contains lots of sick stuff. You have been warned."[12] Second, Judge Cohn questioned the government's involvement in the prosecution:

> The government's enthusiastic beginning petered out to a salvage effort once it recognized that the communications which so alarmed the University of Michigan officials was only a rather savage and tasteless piece of fiction. Why the government became involved in the matter is not really explained in the record. . . . The case would have been better handled as a disciplinary matter, . . . despite whatever difficulties inhere in such a course.[13]

At the conclusion of oral argument, and again at the end of his opinion, Judge Cohn indicated: "[T]he Court is very skeptical, and about the best thing the government's got going for it at this moment is the sincerity of purpose exhibited by [the Assistant United States Attorneys prosecuting the case]. I am not sure that sincerity of purpose is either synonymous with a good case under the law, or even the exercise of good judgment."[14]

In response to the Carnegie Mellon, University of Michigan, and similar controversies and to the *Georgetown Law Journal's* 1995 publication of the Rimm study, *Time* magazine devoted its 3 July 1995 cover story to "Cyberporn!" Before 1995 was out, a federal prosecutor in Munich informed CompuServe, the world's second largest online service provider, that more than 200 Internet newsgroups accessible through CompuServe allegedly violated German law. Threatened with prosecution, CompuServe responded by prohibiting access through its service to all of the identified newsgroups — including discussion groups about homosexuality and sex-related issues. Because newsgroups are accessible without regard for the user's location or nationality, the German prosecutor's action and CompuServe's response had the effect of terminating access to those newsgroups by all of CompuServe's customers located in more than 140 countries. When CompuServe reinstated most of those newsgroups, the Munich prosecutor responded by arresting a CompuServe employee in Germany.

On 1 February 1996 Congress responded to the avalanche of media reports, press releases, studies, and prosecutions lamenting the presence of sexually explicit expression on the Internet by passing the Communications Decency Act.[15] The Act criminalized the knowing use of an "interactive computer system" to transmit or display to a minor "any comment, request, suggestion, proposal, image, or other communication that, in context, depicts or describes, in terms patently offensive as measured by contemporary community standards, sexual or excretory activities or organs."[16] The Act applied not only to the originator of the offending communication, but also to anyone who knowingly permits a telecommunications facility under his or her control to be used for such an activity, irrespective of whether "the user of such service placed the call or initiated the communication."[17]

First introduced in February 1995 by Senator James Exon (D-Nebr.), the legislation appeared unlikely to reach the Senate floor. However, growing concern over sexual expression on the Internet and an aggressive campaign by Senator Exon, who took to the Senate floor with a large blue binder filled with sexually explicit images downloaded from the Internet and dial-up electronic bulletin boards, carried the day. The Justice Department argued that the provision was not necessary and would prove "virtually impossible" to enforce, and constitutional law scholars regarded it as unconstitutional. Harvard law professor Laurence Tribe called it "a frontal assault on the First Amendment."[18] Nevertheless, the Senate, and later the House of Representatives, passed the amendment. On 1 February 1996 it became law as part of the veto-proof Telecommunications Act of 1996. *Time* magazine wrote: "At the end of the debate — which was carried live on C-Span — few Senators wanted to cast a nationally televised vote that might later be characterized as pro-pornography."[19] Before the year was out, a federal court had blocked the law on the grounds that it violated the First Amendment. On 26 June 1997 the U.S. Supreme Court overwhelmingly found the Communications Decency Act to be unconstitutional.

Although media attention and political outrage suggest that "cybersex" dominates the Internet, it does not. Both *Time* and the Rimm study published in the *Georgetown Law Journal* claimed that 83.5% of pictures on newsgroups were sexually explicit. There is ample reason to doubt that statistic. *Time* subsequently published a clarification noting "damaging flaws" in Rimm's research; and both Carnegie Mellon University, at which the research was conducted, and Georgetown University, which published it, formed committees to investigate the research and publication process. Even if that statistic is valid, it ignores the fact that sexually explicit expression accounts for only 3% of all newsgroup messages, and newsgroup messages account for only 11.5% of all Internet traffic; so sexually explicit material makes up only one-third of 1% of Internet traffic. That is a substantially lower percentage of sexually explicit expression than is found in many newsstands, video stores, or premium cable television channels.

Sexual content is available on the Internet primarily from two types of services: newsgroups and web sites. More than 100 newsgroups provide access to a wide range of sexually explicit stories, images, and messages. Most of these newsgroups are part of the "alt" hierarchy; "alt.sex" and "alt.sex.stories" are the largest sexually explicit newsgroups and two of the five largest of all newsgroups. Other "alt.sex" newsgroups run the gamut from "alt.sex. blondes" and "alt.sex.pictures," which tend to feature text and images that might be found in widely available "adult" magazines, such as *Playboy* or *Penthouse,* to groups dedicated to far more extreme topics, such as "alt.sex.bondage," "alt.sex.bestiality," and even "alt.sex.rape." These latter groups are more numerous than those dealing with more mainstream sexual behavior, but they account for fewer postings. Sexually explicit content also is provided under the "alt" hierarchy in groups that feature "binaries" — images, sounds, and video clips — such as "alt.binaries.sounds. erotica" and "alt.binaries.pictures.erotica." The "alt" hierarchy also includes groups such as "alt.sex.abstinence," "alt.sex.safe," "alt. sexual.abuse.recovery," "alt.answers.humansexuality," "alt.politics.sex," "alt.recovery.addiction.sexuality," and "alt.support.disabled.sexuality." As with all of the "alt" newsgroups, these are available without charge to the user; but many servers do not provide access to the groups devoted to more extreme topics.

The other Internet-based source of sexually explicit material includes a wide variety of World Wide Web sites. Some private individuals have web sites that feature such material. However, the majority of sexually explicit sites are either commercial — the online equivalent of "adult" theaters and bookstores — or provided as a public service concerned with safe sex, medical research, literature, or political consciousness-raising. The federal district court that enjoined the government from enforcing the Communications Decency Act noted the variety and the value of sexually explicit expression on the Internet. According to Chief Judge Sloviter, that expression includes not only commercial pornography, which is itself protected by the First Amendment, but also the text of the play, "*Angels in America[,]* which concerns homosex-

17

uality and AIDS portrayed in graphic language," news articles on "the female genital mutilation routinely practiced and officially condoned in some countries," "[p]hotographs appearing in *National Geographic* or a travel magazine of the sculptures in India of couples copulating in numerous positions, a written description of a brutal prison rape, or Francis Clemente's painting 'Labirinth.'"[20]

Despite the relatively low proportion of sexually explicit expression on the Internet, it is an important topic for inquiry and debate, especially among educators. Although accounting for a tiny percentage of Internet traffic, the sexually explicit stories, images, and movies that are available on the Internet span a very wide range, which includes graphic and often violent material. While the accessibility of this material to children is limited, as is discussed in detail below, the technologies involved are often more familiar to children than to their parents and other adults. And that accessibility will only increase as Congress and the President rush to expand Internet access in classrooms and libraries. However, the most important reason that the debate over sexually explicit expression on the Internet is valuable is because this is where virtually all efforts to regulate Internet expression are focused; this is where the limits of free expression are being tested today.

Notes

1. *See generally* American Civil Liberties Union v. Reno, 929 F. Supp. 824, at 831-32 (E.D. Pa. 1996), *aff'd,* Reno v. American Civil Liberties Union, _ U.S. _, 1997 U.S. LEXIS 4037 (1997).
2. Larry Irving, "Equipping Our Children with the Tools to Compete Successfully in the New Economy," remarks to the Conference on Technology and the Schools: Preparing the New Workforce for the 21st Century, Randolph Center, Vt., 28 October 1996 (http://www. ntia.doc.gov.ntiahome/speeches/1028961i_vermont.html).
3. Stephanie Schorow, "Education Upgrade: State Program Links School Computers With Internet Access," *Boston Herald*, 25 October 1996, p. O43.

4. "Clinton Begins Push for School Computers," *Los Angeles Times*, 9 February 1997, p. A23.
5. American Library Association, *How Many Libraries Are on the Internet?* (September 1996) (http://www.ala.org/library/fact26.html).
6. Marty Rimm, "Marketing Pornography on the Information Superhighway," *Georgetown Law Journal* 83 (1995): 1849.
7. *Proposed Policy for Providing Access to Networked Electronic Resources*, Carnegie Mellon University, 19 June 1995.
8. Letter from Erwin R. Steinberg, chair of the bulletin board committee, to Robert Mehrabian, president of Carnegie Mellon University, 19 June 1995.
9. 18 U.S.C. § 875(c) (1988). Baker was indicted for allegedly transmitting a threat, even though the transmission constituted a story, signed by the author, giving his correct e-mail address, posted to a publicly accessible Internet newsgroup that featured only fantasy stories concerning sex, and seeking feedback from readers.
10. J. White, "Student Judged 'Too Dangerous' to be Released," *Michigan Daily*, 13 February 1995, p. A1 (quoting Judge Bernard Friedman).
11 United States v. Baker, Crim. No. 95-80106 (E.D. Mich. 21 June 1995).
12. Jake Baker, "Doe," posted to alt.sex.stories on 9 January 1995. The name of the story has been altered to protect the identity of the student named in the story. "Jake Baker," authorities also learned, was not the defendant's real name.
13. United States v. Baker, Crim. No. 95-80106 (citations omitted).
14. Id.
15. Telecommunications Competition and Deregulation Act of 1996, S. 652, 104th Cong., 2nd Sess. §§ 501 *et seq.*
16. Id. § 502(e).
17. Id. § 502(d).
18. Philip Elmer-Dewitt, "On a Screen Near You: Cyberporn," *Time*, 3 July 1995, p. 42 (quoting Harvard law professor Laurence Tribe).
19. Id.
20. American Civil Liberties Union v. Reno, 929 F. Supp. 824, 853 (E.D. Pa. 1996) (Sloviter, C.J., concurring), aff'd, ___U.S. ___, 1997 U.S. LEXIS 4037 (1997).

CHAPTER TWO

LEGAL ISSUES
AND THE INTERNET

The proliferation of Internet-based services presents many legal issues that are the subject of extensive, ongoing discussions. Although only one set of those issues — dealing with the regulation of sexually explicit expression — is the subject of this book, an understanding of the Internet requires some familiarity with the broad range of issues it poses. Moreover, it is impossible to evaluate the significance of the accessibility of sexually explicit material through the Internet, much less propose approaches to the problem, without understanding the broader context in which that issue occurs. Legal issues concerning the Internet may be divided generally into five categories.

Application of the First Amendment

The first set of issues posed by information technologies concerns the application to electronic expression of the First Amendment to the U.S. Constitution, which provides that "Congress shall make no law . . . abridging the freedom of speech, or of the press." Beginning with its earliest free-expression cases, the Supreme Court has found that the protection afforded by the First Amendment depends on the medium of communication involved. When traditional media, such as newspapers, books, and pickets, are involved, the Court has interpreted the First Amendment to prevent the government from restricting expression prior to its utterance or publication or merely because the government disagrees with the sentiment expressed,[1] from making impermissible distinctions based on content,[2] or compelling speech or granting access to the expressive capacity of another without demonstrating that the abridgment is narrowly tailored to serve a compelling governmental interest.[3]

However, when the government sought to impose similar restrictions on newer media, such as sound trucks, telephones, or broadcast television, the Court has assumed that "differences in the characteristics of new media justify differences in the First Amendment standards applied to them."[4] In *Kovacs* v. *Cooper*, a case involving a New Jersey statute forbidding the use of a "loud and raucous" sound truck, Justice Jackson wrote in support of the ordinance's constitutionality:

> I do not agree that, if we sustain regulations or prohibitions of sound trucks, they must therefore be valid if applied to other methods of "communication of ideas." The moving picture screen, the radio, the newspaper, the handbill, the sound truck and the street corner orator have differing natures, values, abuses and dangers. Each, in my view, is a law unto itself.[5]

What is the law applicable to digital information, which shares characteristics of many different media? This issue has been at the center of recent disputes in the United States over legislation attempting to regulate sexually explicit expression on the Internet. The government has argued that the Internet is like over-the-air broadcasting and therefore subject to the same restraints as broadcasters. First Amendment advocates have argued, and so far the courts have agreed, that the First Amendment should apply to the Internet with the same force with which it applies to print media.[6] The resolution of this question goes to the heart of the scope of free expression to be permitted on the Internet and is discussed in greater detail below.

Intellectual Property

The second category of issues includes those dealing with the ownership of electronic information and the application of existing intellectual property laws to the Internet. The technologies involved may distort the application of existing law. For example, the monopoly rights of copyright owners and the incentive those rights create to author and distribute original expression is altered by the rapidly growing prominence of electronic information networks. U.S. intellectual property law was designed for a world in which copying was difficult, economically impractical, and relatively easy to regulate by focusing on the physical object and centralized "copying centers." When information is digital and readily available through networks and the technologies to copy are widespread, affordable, and highly effective, intellectual property law is challenged.

In 1993 the Clinton Administration formed an Intellectual Property Rights Working Group, chaired by Assistant Secretary of Commerce for Patents and Trademarks Bruce Lehman, to examine the impact of information networks on intellectual property rights and to recommend legislative changes to address those issues. The working group's report, *Intellectual Property and the National Information Infrastructure,* was released in September 1995 and highlights the difficult copyright issues presented by information networks.

For example, the report argues that the right to reproduce a copyrighted work, perhaps the most fundamental right protected by copyright law, is implicated in nearly every Internet transaction. The report sets out the following examples of when a work is copied and therefore when, in the absence of fair use or other defense, an infringement of the reproduction right has taken place:

- When a work is put into a computer, whether on a disk, diskette, ROM, or other storage device or in RAM for more than a very brief period.[7]
- When a printed work is "scanned" into a digital file.

23

- When other works — including photographs, motion pictures, or sound recordings — are digitized.
- Whenever a digitized file is "uploaded" from a user's computer to a bulletin board system ["BBS"] or other server.
- Whenever a digitized file is "downloaded" from a BBS or other server.
- When a file is transferred from one computer network user to another.[8]

Another important right protected by copyright law is the right to distribute a work. However, that right is substantially circumscribed by the "first sale" doctrine set out in Section 109(a) of the 1976 Act, under which the owner of a lawfully obtained copy is entitled to sell, give, lend, rent, or otherwise dispose of that copy without the copyright owner's permission. This doctrine limits copyright owners' rights by making only the initial distribution of a particular copy of a copyrighted work subject to their control.

The first sale doctrine's importance in the Internet context should not be underestimated: If a transaction by which a user obtains a "copy" of a work is characterized as a "distribution," then the user may be entitled to make additional distributions without the copyright owner's permission and without liability for infringement. However, the working group's report argues that most "distributions" of works by means of computer networks result in a new copy being made, rather than the original copy being handed on to someone else; these are "reproductions," rather than "distributions." New reproductions are not permitted by the first sale doctrine. This type of dissemination-by-reproduction violates the copyright owner's exclusive rights to distribute and to reproduce. As a result, while U.S. copyright law permits one user to give to another a physical copy of a copyrighted book, the law appears to prohibit that user from transmitting an electronic copy of that same book.

A third example of the serious effect of electronic information networks on intellectual property rights concerns the exclusive right of the copyright owner to perform or display his or her work.

When a digital file is transmitted over wires or satellite signals so that users with the requisite hardware and software might view it, then, under the current law, a "performance" or "display" has occurred. The "public" nature of a performance or display — which brings it within the scope of copyright law — is defined sufficiently broadly to apply to multiple individual viewers who may watch a work being performed or displayed in a variety of locations at different times. Thus, according to the working group's report, when a user visually "browses" through copies of works on a network or computer bulletin board or other electronic resource, a public performance or display occurs.

Digital technologies may alter the legal calculus for what constitutes "fair use." Determining which uses are "fair," and therefore permitted under U.S. law without the copyright holder's permission, depends in large part on whether there is a market for the portion of a work copied. Recently, courts have been limiting what uses are fair by focusing on the potential, future markets for expression presented by electronic networks and on the availability — again, often electronically — of smaller sections of articles and books.[9] A use such as copying a page from an article might previously have been thought fair, because it involved copying only a portion of a larger work where there was no market for that portion alone. Today, however, such a use would likely be found to be unfair because chapters, paragraphs, and even sentences are available, or will be available, online and therefore their uncompensated use affects an existing or future market. As computers create markets in smaller and smaller fragments of works, uses that were fair in print may cease to be so in the context of digital information.

Most important, the Internet may distort the constitutional requirement that copyright law protect only fixed expression, not facts or ideas. The Clinton Administration task force's intellectual property report blurs the line between expression, which is protected, and substantive content, which is not, by limiting users' ability to access digital information. The Supreme Court stressed in *Feist Publications, Inc.* v. *Rural Telephone Service Company* that "[t]he most fundamental axiom of copyright law is that '[n]o author may copyright his ideas or the facts he narrates.'. . . [C]opyright assures authors the right to their original expression, but encourages others to build freely upon the ideas and information conveyed by a work."[10] The Court therefore held unanimously that a compilation of facts, such as a database, can be copyrighted only "if it features an original selection or arrangement of facts," but that "[i]n no event may copyright extend to the facts themselves."[11]

The danger that copyright law may be misapplied to protect facts and ideas — information, not just expression — is particularly great in the electronic context. Given the working group's conclusions that a digital work may not be transmitted, uploaded, downloaded, printed, displayed, or performed without violating the exclusive rights of the copyright holder, copyright holders may have an effective monopoly over facts or ideas that are expressed in digital form. Although the law is designed to protect only expression, the law inadvertently protects underlying facts and ideas in digital contexts, because they cannot be accessed without illegally accessing the protected expression at the same time. Thus any information — no matter whether a fact or idea or even work in the public domain — that is available only or primarily in electronic form may be inaccessible to the public unless Congress or the courts clarify the application of copyright law in the digital environment.[12]

The resolution of copyright issues is relevant to the debate over children's access to sexually explicit expression, especially because much of such expression on the Internet is illegally copied from magazines and videos. The Newsgroups Info Center, which provides information on the structure and use of newsgroups, describes those groups featuring sexually explicit photos as "[g]igabytes of copyright violations."[13] In fact, one of the first online copyright cases was brought by Playboy Enterprises against a bulletin board operator who provided access to unauthorized copies of *Playboy* photographs.[14] Increasingly, the creators of sexually explicit expression are charging for online access to their content. Those creators therefore are trying to enforce their copyrights against Internet users who illegally reproduce and distribute that material. The enforcement of copyrights on the Internet is certain to decrease the availability of sexually explicit expression to children.

Economic Issues

The third category of issues concerns how electronic information networks are paid for and how hospitable they are to commercial services. At present, most publicly available forms of two-way communication, such as telephone and mail, are regulated by national governments. Often, these regulations set forth the terms under which service must be provided, establish basic principles of nondiscrimination among customers, and govern, either directly or indirectly, the rates that may be charged and the profits that may be taken. The Internet is a notable exception. Although a user may pay a fee to a local Internet service provider to access the Internet, no charge is assessed for using the Internet itself and there is no regulation of its economic health or quality of service. The Internet is unique among communications media in not levying a charge based on distance, duration, time, or message size. A telephone call from Washington to London is subject to regulated tariffs based on the duration and time of the call. But an electronic message, or even a digital telephone call, transmitted through the Internet is "free" to the user. This is a key reason why politicians and school administrators have found the Internet so attractive for education.

These features have prompted questions about the long-term stability of the Internet and interest in facilitating the rapid deployment of Internet-based commercial services as a likely source of future financial support and improved content. Until recently, the Internet has been dominated by free material of often uncertain provenance, accuracy, and reliability. Commercial services have largely been limited to promotional and information roles until effective means of paying for goods online are developed. Credit cards have thus far proved a limited solution, because of fears that data will be intercepted. As a result, while some users provide credit card information online, many online service providers allow the user to order on the Internet and then call using the public telephone network to provide payment information. Providing for secure online payment systems is critical to commercial use of the Internet and to its long-term financial stability. Such systems also are facilitating the commercialization of online sexually explicit expression, which reduces the accessibility of such information to children.

Privacy, Security, and Encryption

The fourth set of issues presented by the Internet includes the privacy of individuals, the security of data in the computer or on the network, and the availability of encryption software to protect data in the event they are intercepted. In this context, privacy refers to controlling the dissemination and use of data, including both information that is knowingly disclosed and that which is revealed unintentionally. Privacy is among the most hotly debated topics in Washington and other national capitals today. Almost 1,000 of the 7,945 bills introduced in the 104th Congress addressed some privacy issue, and this level of political activity is reflected throughout much of the world, especially in Europe.[15]

More data than ever before are made available in the digital format, which is easier and less expensive than nondigital data to access, manipulate, and store. And more data are generated in the first place, because of the ease and very low cost of doing so and because of the high value of data in an increasingly information-based society. As a result, others know more about you — even things you may not know about yourself — than ever before. According to a 1994 estimate, U.S. computers alone hold more than five billion records, trading information on every man, woman, and child an average of five times every day. Just one industry — credit reporting — accounts for 400 million credit files, which are updated with more than two *billion* entries every month and which facilitate 1.5 million credit decisions every day.[16] The ramifications of such a readily accessible storehouse of electronic information are astonishing. Consider this catalogue from the *New York Times Sunday Magazine* of the data that are routinely collected about you:

- Your health history, credit history, marital history, educational history, travel history, and employment history.
- The times and telephone numbers of every call you make and receive.
- The magazines you subscribe to and the books you borrow from the library.
- Your cash withdrawals.
- All of your purchases by credit card or check. In the not-so-distant future, when electronic cash becomes the rule, even the purchases you still make by bills and coins could be logged.
- What you eat. Data from supermarket scanners are tracked for marketing purposes.
- Your electronic mail.
- Where you go and what you see on the World Wide Web.[17]

The growth of the Internet, the dramatic increase in the volume of data generated and recorded, and the ease and comparatively low cost with which those data are collected, manipulated, and stored has prompted increased concern not only with privacy but also with security and encryption.

Security refers to the integrity of the data storage, processing, and transmission systems and includes issues about the reliability of the hardware and software, the protections against intrusion into or theft of the computer equipment, and the resistance of computer systems from being infiltrated by unpermitted users ("hacking"). Encryption is the practice of encoding data so that even if a computer or network is compromised, the data's content will remain secret. Security and encryption issues are important because they are central to public confidence in networks and to the use of the systems for sensitive or secret data, such as the processing of information touching on national security. These issues are surprisingly controversial, because of governments' interest in preventing digital information from being impervious to official interception and decoding for law enforcement and other purposes. In the United States, encryption software is treated as a "munition" and therefore is subject to government regulation.

Privacy, security, and encryption affect the availability of sexually explicit information on the Internet because of the role the apparent anonymity and confidentiality of Internet transactions play in facilitating the distribution of such expression. Anecdotal evidence suggests that many people either create or access sexual material on the Internet because they can do so without venturing into the public eye. Although the privacy of Internet transactions is largely illusory, the perception that such privacy exists is important to many Internet users. The threat of routine monitoring of Internet use is likely to significantly reduce access to sexually explicit images and text.

Multinational Impact and Regulation

The fifth category of legal issues posed by information networks concerns the multinational character of those networks. Digital information is inherently global: It respects no boundaries. Anne Branscomb has written: "[t]he very existence of information technology is threatening to nation states."[18] And Joseph Pelton has noted that information technologies and services may very well be "rendering the nation state obsolete."[19]

Whether in a wire or optical fiber or beamed from a satellite or microwave dish, information — particularly electronic information — is ubiquitous. Unlike a truckload of steel or a freight train of coal, television and radio signals, telephone, facsimile, and modem communications are difficult to pinpoint and almost impossible to block through either legal or technological means. "[D]igital information flowing in cables or moving through space will be, in effect, a single, homogenous stream . . . [I]t will become increasingly impossible to maintain any of the traditional distinctions between transmissions carrying news, entertainment, financial data or even personal phone calls."[20]

As a result of its inherently transnational character, information has been the subject of some of the earliest multinational agreements, treaties, and organizations. Binational postal treaties were concluded as early as 1601 between France and Spain and 1670 between France and England. The Postal Congress of Berne in 1874 established a multinational postal regime — administered today by the Universal Postal Union — 74 years before the General Agreement on Tariffs and Trade was opened for signature. This global framework is so comprehensive, and the practical difficulty of separating domestic and international mail so great, that UPU regulations today set the terms for domestic as well as international service.

Electronically transmitted information also prompted multinational agreements almost immediately upon its commercial deployment. The telegraph was first employed commercially in the early 1840s, and by 1849 bilateral and multinational agreements were in place to facilitate and regulate its transnational use. In 1865 Napoleon III called an international conference in Paris to address technical standards, codes, and tariffs for the telegraph. The 20 countries attending negotiated the first International Telegraph Union, which later combined with the Radiotelegraph Conference to form the International Telecommunication Union. In short, by the time the telephone appeared on the scene in 1876, there already existed an 11-year-old structure for dealing with multinational electronic communication.

Governments have been less far-sighted in dealing with the implications of the current information revolution. While talks are under way in some multinational forums, such as the World Intellectual Property Organization and the European Union, national law continues to be the principal recourse for regulators. As a result, information networks and databases are subject not only to the laws of the jurisdiction in which they are located, but also to the laws of the jurisdiction in which they are received. For information resources available via Internet, that involves 190 nations, as well as state or territorial laws.

This poses a particular challenge when thinking about sexually explicit expression, because that expression is outlawed in many countries. In fact, while there are many national and multinational guarantees of freedom of expression, the United States stands virtually alone in the community of nations in the amount and diversity of expression its laws protect.[21] Because almost any material on the Internet is accessible around the world, suppliers of sexually explicit content must be concerned with whether their material will violate laws outside of the United States. This is particularly true for multinational businesses and organizations, which may have offices, personnel, or assets that can be seized by foreign regulators. This concern has contributed to suppliers restricting access to sexually explicit expression by requiring a password or subscription. On the other hand, the inherently global nature of the Internet calls into question whether national content regulations can ever be wholly effective, particularly against not-for-profit and anonymous content providers, since content outlawed in one country may nonetheless be accessed by servers in other countries.

Collectively, questions about Internet content regulation, intellectual property protection, payment systems, privacy, and jurisdiction both directly affect the availability of online sexually explicit material and form the backdrop against which the laws applicable to such expression must be considered. The next chapter addresses the U.S. laws applicable to sexual expression generally and the extent to which the First Amendment restrains the creation and enforcement of such laws.

Notes

1. R.A.V. v. City of St. Paul, 505 U.S. 377 (1992); New York Times Company v. United States, 403 U.S. 713 (1971).
2. R.A.V., 505 U.S. 377; Texas v. Johnson, 491 U.S. 397 (1989); Consolidated Edison Company v. Public Service Commission, 447 U.S. 530 (1980).
3. Wooley v. Maynard, 430 U.S. 705 (1977); Miami Herald Publishing Company v. Tornillo, 418 U.S. 241, 244 (1974); West Virginia State Board of Education v. Barnette, 319 U.S. 624 (1943).

4. Red Lion Broadcasting Company v. Federal Communications Commission, 395 U.S. 367, 386 (1969).

5. 336 U.S. 77, 97 (1949). (Jackson, J., concurring). *See also* Turner Broadcasting System, Inc. v. Federal Communications Commission, 512 U.S. 662, 639 (1994); City of Los Angeles v. Preferred Communications, Inc., 476 U.S. 488, 496 (1986); Federal Communications Commission v. League of Women Voters of California, 468 U.S. 364, 374 (1984); Members of the City Council of Los Angeles v. Taxpayers for Vincent, 466 U.S. 789, 818 (1984).

6. Reno v. American Civil Liberties Union, _ U.S. _, 1997 U.S. LEXIS 4037 (1997).

7. RAM means "random access memory" and is the computer's active, "thinking" memory. RAM must be constantly "refreshed" by electric current to retain its digital content. RAM is erased when a computer is turned off. ROM means "read-only memory." Unlike RAM, it is not erased when the computer in which it is installed is turned off, because its digital information is permanently on a chip.

8. *Intellectual Property and the National Information Infrastructure: The Report of the Working Group on Intellectual Property Rights* (Washington, D.C.: Information Infrastructure Task Force, 1995).

9. *See, for example,* American Geophysical Union v. Texaco, 37 F.3d 881 (2d Cir. 1994).

10. Feist Publications, Inc. v. Rural Telephone Service Company, 499 U.S. 340, 344-45, 349 (1991).

11. Id., p. 351.

12. Fred H. Cate, "The Technological Transformation of Copyright Law," *Iowa Law Review* 81 (1996): 1395.

13. Kevin Atkinson, Newsgroups Info Center (1995) (available at http://sunsite.unc.edu/pub/docs/about-the-net/usenet-info-center/report/txt/ul-abriv.txt).

14. Playboy Enterprises v. Frena, 839 F. Supp. 1552, 1559 (M.D. Fla. 1993).

15. Fred H. Cate, *Privacy in the Information Age* (Washington, D.C.: Brookings Institution Press, 1997).

16. Steven A. Bibas, "A Contractual Approach to Data Privacy," *Harvard Journal of Law and Public Policy* 17 (1994): 591, 593; 142 Congressional Record Sl 1,868 (30 September 1996) (statement of Mr. Bryan).

17. James Gleick, "Behind Closed Doors: Big Brother Is Us," *New York Times Sunday Magazine*, 29 September 1996, p. 130.

18. Anne W. Branscomb, "Global Governance of Global Networks: A Survey of Transborder Data Flow in Transition," *Vanderbilt Law Review* 36 (1983): 985, 987. See generally Fred H. Cate, "Global Information Policymaking and Domestic Law," *Indiana Journal of Global Legal Studies* (1994): 467.

19. Joseph N. Pelton, "The Globalization of Universal Telecommunications Services," *Annual Review of the Institute for Information Studies* (1991): 141, 143.

20. W. Sparks, Address to the Conference on World Communications, Annenberg School for Communication, University of Pennsylvania, May 1980, *quoted in* Branscomb, "Global Governance of Global Networks," p. 1006.

21. *See, for example,* Universal Declaration of Human Rights, G.A. Res. 217A (III), U.N. GAOR, 3rd Sess., U.N. Doc. A/810 (1948); European Convention for the Protection of Human Rights and Fundamental Freedoms, art. 10(1), signed 4 November 1950, 213 U.N.T.S. 221; International Covenant on Civil and Political Rights, art. 19(2), opened for signature 19 December 1966, 999 U.N.T.S. 171 (entered into force 23 March 1976); African Charter on Human and Peoples' Rights, art. 9, opened for signature 26 June 1981, 21 I.L.M. 59 (entered into force 21 October 1986); American Convention on Human Rights, art. 13, opened for signature 22 November 1969, 1144 U.N.T.S. 123 (entered into force 18 July 1978).

CHAPTER THREE

THE FIRST AMENDMENT AND SEXUALLY EXPLICIT EXPRESSION

The First Amendment to the U.S. Constitution extends extra-ordinary protection to expression. But for all of its power, that constitutional provision is frequently misunderstood. Although we often speak of the "right" to free speech, the First Amendment actually accords no rights at all. Rather, it denies to the government the power to interfere with the expression of its citizens. The reasons that jurists and scholars have identified for it doing so, and the practical effect of the limits the First Amendment imposes on the government, are important to understanding the limits imposed on efforts to regulate sexually explicit material on the Internet.

Introduction to the First Amendment

The core meaning of the First Amendment, according to the Supreme Court, is protecting expression relating to self-governance.[1] Expression concerning the activities of the government and elected and appointed officials is critical and protected by the First Amendment because it is the information that the citizens of a democratic society must have to govern. This right expresses the most foundational of values in American society. As former Judge Robert Bork has written:

The First Amendment indicates that there is something special about speech. We would know that much even without a first amendment, for the entire structure of the Constitution creates a representative democracy, a form of government that would be meaningless without freedom to discuss government and its policies. Freedom for political speech could and should be inferred even if there were no First Amendment.[2]

But self-governance is not the limit of the First Amendment. Even though it defines self-governance expression very broadly, the Supreme Court has extended the First Amendment far beyond self-governance. The Court has often asserted that the First Amendment "was fashioned to assure the unfettered interchange of ideas for the bringing about of political and social changes desired by the people."[3] Under this concept of a speech "marketplace," the "remedy" for dangerous expression is more and varied expression.[4]

One might reasonably ask what danger there is that ideas might be lost by restricting sexually explicit expression on the Internet. But the marketplace metaphor countenances not only that what is accepted as "truth" will likely change over time, but also the context of what is accepted as taste. Martin Redish has referred, in the context of scientific knowledge, to the "principle of epistemological humility." "This principle posits that whatever the currently prevailing beliefs may be, history teaches us that scientific or moral advances may at some future point make those beliefs appear either silly or monstrous."[5] Certainly, history teaches of dramatic change in what is accepted within the social norm. Compare even the most moderate elements of modern society with those of New England under the Puritans or of England during Victorian times. Past practices concerning dress, social etiquette, and the treatment of women that appear so "silly or monstrous" today were once some societies' prevailing beliefs. "Certainty is generally illusion," Justice Holmes wrote 100 years ago, "and repose is not the destiny of man."[6]

Expression may be regulated only because of the tangible harm it causes and certainly not because the government disagrees with the expression. "If there is a bedrock principle underlying the First Amendment," Justice Brennan wrote for the Court in 1989, "it is that the Government may not prohibit the expression of an idea simply because society finds the idea itself offensive or disagreeable."[7] It is for this reason that the government may prohibit an act, such as murder, but is powerless to restrict expression about that act. As Rodney Smolla has written, "[w]hile the First Amendment is not an absolute, the neutrality principle is. Modern First Amendment cases establish a *per se* rule making the punishment of speech flatly unconstitutional if the penalty is based on the offensiveness or the undesirability of the viewpoint expressed."[8]

As a result, Congress, prosecutors, and courts are forbidden from sanctioning expression merely because it conveys an idea, advocates an action, or reflects a vision of society that they find reprehensible. Instead, under the marketplace principle, expression may be regulated only because of the tangible harm it causes and, even then, only with the greatest care and restraint. In fact, under the Supreme Court's application of the marketplace principle, the preferred "remedy" for dangerous expression is more, healthier expression. "Under the First Amendment there is no such thing as a false idea. However pernicious an opinion may seem, we depend for its correction not on the consciences of judges and juries but on the competition of other ideas."[9]

This is true even though the government or the society finds the expression offensive or contentious.[10] In *Terminello* v. *Chicago,* Justice Douglas wrote for the Court that free speech "may indeed best serve its high purpose when it induces a condition of unrest, creates dissatisfaction with conditions as they are, or even stirs people to anger. It may strike at prejudices and preconceptions and have profound unsettling effects."[11] The Court recognized this in *Stanley* v. *Georgia,* when it wrote that the Constitution's protection of expression "is not confined to the expression of ideas that are conventional or shared by the majority."[12]

Courts also have recognized the First Amendment importance of, and intrinsic link between, freedom of thought and self-expression. That expression may be offensive to others, but for the government to suppress it intrudes deeply on human identity and, in the words of David Richardson, "the notion of self-respect that comes from a mature person's full and untrammeled exercise of capacities central to human rationality."[13] Thomas Emerson has written that "suppression of belief, opinion, or other expression is an affront to the dignity of man, a negation of man's essential nature."[14] Under this self-fulfillment rationale, the value of free expression is not felt only by the originator of the expression. Society as a whole may benefit, particularly if the opportunity for expression ameliorates the likelihood of acting on antisocial ideas. Moreover, the expression of antisocial ideas provides an opportunity to respond to those ideas with other expression or with nongovernmental activity.

Suppression of individual thought and expression may threaten the stability of society itself. Justice Brandeis wrote in *Whitney* v. *California*:

> [I]t is hazardous to discourage thought, hope and imagination; that fear breeds repression; that repression breeds hate; that hate menaces stable government; that the path of safety lies in the opportunity to discuss freely supposed grievances and proposed remedies; and that the fitting remedy of evil counsels is good ones.[15]

By limiting the ability of individuals to convince others of their ideas through spoken or written advocacy, laws curbing free expression may encourage discontent and violence and certainly deny society the opportunity to prevent them. Suppressing expression may give the illusion that the ideas no longer exist, but it does not lead to the eradication of the antisocial deeds advocated.

Society also benefits in the long run through better, more fully developed, more socialized members. The "fulfillment" of uninhibited expression, therefore, is shared beyond the expression's originator. Rodney Smolla has written:

> The fulfillment that comes from speech is bonded to man's capacity to think, imagine, and create. Conscience and consciousness are the sacred precincts of mind and soul. The

linkage of speech to thought, to man's central capacity to reason and wonder, is what places speech above other forms of fulfillment, and beyond the routine jurisdiction of the state. . . .

The First Amendment both protects and provokes the expressive spirit. On its surface it is a negative restraint on government. But beneath the surface lies a more vexing voice, one that affirmatively *encourages* Americans to speak, to take stands, to demand to be heard, to demand to *participate*.[16]

To deny that fulfillment and that right to participate, even when an individual's contribution is distasteful and disturbing, is something that a democratic society should not countenance.

Finally, the First Amendment protects expression because of the difficulties inherent in even the best-intentioned effort to regulate speech. For example, how are the lines between acceptable and unacceptable expression to be drawn? In *Cohen* v. *California*, Justice Harlan wrote for the Supreme Court:

How is one to distinguish this [phrase "Fuck the Draft" worn on the defendant's jacket] from any other offensive word? Surely the State has no right to clean public debate to the point where it is grammatically palatable to the most squeamish among us. Yet no readily ascertainable general principle exists for stopping short of that result were we to affirm the judgment below. For, while the particular four-letter word being litigated here is perhaps more distasteful than most others of its genre, it is nevertheless often true that one man's vulgarity is another's lyric.[17]

The difficulties surrounding drawing those lines also contribute to the problem of self-censorship. If you do not know for what expression you may be held liable, you are less likely to create or transmit any questionable expression. This tendency to "steer clear" of potentially illegal speech has caused the Supreme Court to protect expression that it believes may not independently warrant protection. In *New York Times Company* v. *Sullivan*, Justice Brennan wrote for the Court that the "erroneous statement is inevitable in free debate, and . . . must be protected if the freedoms of expression are to have the 'breathing space' that they 'need . . . to survive.'"[18]

Similarly, the First Amendment acts as a restraint on the natural tendency to censor. Everyone has some expression they would like to prohibit; and once the government begins targeting expression for suppression, it is unlikely to stop. This is certainly the regrettable lesson of history. The invention of a commercially viable printing press in the late 15th century brought with it the professional censor. Pope Alexander VI issued a bull in 1501 forbidding printing without a license, and in 1559 the first *Index Expurgatorious* was issued. Germany instituted censorship in 1529. By the time the mob overran the Bastille in 1789, more than 800 authors, printers, and book dealers had been imprisoned there.

The human penchant for seeking to silence ideas and speakers with which and with whom we do not agree, or that merely threaten our quietude, is precisely what the First Amendment restrains. It is all too easy to act from self-interest, or to target expression because it is an effective, and often far less expensive, alternative to addressing the real issues that the expression merely signals. The First Amendment limits the power of the government to restrict expression in no small part because it is simply unable to do so with consistency, predictability, and restraint.

The practical effect of a broad, powerful, and central First Amendment is that the Supreme Court interprets it to prevent the government from restricting expression prior to its utterance or publication or merely because the government disagrees with the sentiment expressed.[19] It also forbids the government to make distinctions based on the content of expression, to compel one to speak, or to force someone to grant access to the expression of another, unless the government can demonstrate that its action is narrowly tailored to serve a compelling governmental interest.[20] These First Amendment principles restrict not merely Congress, but all federal and state governmental agencies.[21] This is especially important because most legal restraints on sexually explicit expression occur at the state level. In addition, these First Amendment principles apply to expression that the Court has determined does not independently warrant protection (such as false or defamatory expression),[22] to conduct that involves no speech (such as burning a flag or picketing),[23] and to activities that are ancillary to expression (such as funding and distributing expression).[24]

This last point is particularly important for such organizations as libraries and book stores, which distribute expression that they do not originate or control. Under the Supreme Court's interpretation of the First Amendment, a distributor of publications is not liable for their content unless it either knows or had reason to know that the content was harmful. "[T]he constitutional guarantees of the freedom of speech and of the press stand in the way of imposing" strict liability on distributors for the contents of the reading materials they carry.[25] In *Smith* v. *California,* the Court struck down an ordinance that imposed liability on booksellers for possessing obscene books without requiring that the bookseller know of the books' content. The Court reasoned that "[e]very bookseller would be placed under an obligation to make himself aware of the contents of every book in his shop. It would be altogether unreasonable to demand so near an approach to omniscience."[26] Moreover, the Court stressed, imposing liability on booksellers without a knowledge requirement would necessarily restrict the amount and variety of material available to the public:

> For if the bookseller is criminally liable without knowledge of the contents, . . . he will tend to restrict the books he sells to those he has inspected; and thus the State will have imposed a restriction upon the distribution of constitutionally protected as well as obscene literature. . . . And the bookseller's burden would become the public's burden, for by restricting him[,] the public's access to reading matter would be restricted . . . . [H]is timidity in the face of his absolute criminal liability, thus would tend to restrict the public's access to forms of the printed word which the State could not constitutionally suppress directly. The bookseller's self-censorship, compelled by the State, would be a censorship affecting the whole public, hardly less virulent for being privately administered. Through it, the distribution of all books, both obscene and not obscene, would be impeded.[27]

Obscenity

Despite the extraordinary breadth of the First Amendment, the Supreme Court has found that the amendment's protection does not extend to the distribution or public exhibition of sexually explicit expression that is "obscene." In 1957 in *Roth* v. *United States,* the Court held that "obscenity is not within the area of constitutionally protected speech or press."[28] Although the Court declined to provide a specific definition for "obscenity," its analysis focused on whether the average person, applying contemporary community standards, would find that the dominant theme of the material taken as a whole appealed to "prurient" interests.

Roth set off more than a decade of judicial confusion and indecision about the definition of obscenity, leading the late Justice Stewart to write in 1964 that an intelligent definition might be impossible, but "I know it when I see it."[29] On 31 occasions, the Court reviewed purportedly obscene material and rendered a judgment as to its permissibility.[30] Justice Brennan complained that the examination of this material was "hardly a source of edification to the members of this Court . . . [and] has cast us in the role of an unreviewable board of censorship for the 50 states."[31] In 1966, in a plurality opinion, the Court narrowed the definition of "obscenity" by requiring that lower courts find to be obscene only works that are "*utterly* without redeeming social value."[32] Still, the definition of obscenity lacked the clarity needed to provide the meaningful guidance to citizens and local governments that ultimately would reduce the Court's role as a national board of censorship.

In 1973 the Court finally adopted a specific, albeit still subjective, definition of obscenity. In *Miller* v. *California,* a 5-4 majority held that works are obscene, and therefore outside the protection of the First Amendment, only if 1) "the average person, applying contemporary community standards" would find that the work, taken as a whole, appeals to the prurient interest; 2) the work depicts or describes, in a patently offensive way, sexual or excretory conduct specifically defined by the applicable state law; and 3) the work, taken as a whole, lacks serious literary, artistic, political, or scientific value.[33] The "prurient interest" requirement, the Court later ruled, is satisfied only by expression that does more than "provoke[] only normal, healthy sexual desires."[34] In *Miller* and subsequent cases, the Court stressed that the first two prongs of the test could be judged under subjective local or state community standards. "People in different States vary in their tastes and attitudes, and this diversity is not to be strangled by the absolutism of imposed uniformity," Chief Justice Burger wrote for the Court in *Miller*.[35] There cannot be "fixed, uniform national standards of precisely what appeals to the 'prurient interest' or is 'patently offensive.' . . . [O]ur nation is simply too big and too diverse for this Court to reasonably expect that such standards could be articulated for all 50 states in a single formulation."[36] Redeeming literary, artistic, political, or scientific value, on the other hand, is not a subject for local standards and must therefore be judged under a national "reasonable person" standard.[37]

Contemporaneously with the *Roth-Miller* line of cases, which dealt with distributing and displaying publicly obscene material, the Court also decided *Stanley* v. *Georgia*, which involved the possession of obscenity.[38] In *Stanley* the Court held, without dissent, that the Constitution protected the possession of sexually explicit material, even if it was legally obscene. While the "[s]tates retain broad power to regulate obscenity," Justice Marshall wrote for the Court, "that power simply does not extend to mere possession by the individual in the privacy of his own home."[39] The Court based its decision both on the "right to receive information and ideas, regardless of their social worth," which Justice Marshall wrote "is fundamental to our free society," and on the "right to be free, except in very limited circumstances, from unwanted governmental intrusion into one's privacy."[40] Characterizing the Georgia law at issue in the case, which criminalized possession of obscene material, as a "drastic invasion of personal liberties guaranteed by the First and Fourteenth Amendments," the Court concluded: "If the First Amendment means anything, it means that a State has no business telling a man, sitting alone in his own house, what books he may read or what films he may watch. Our whole constitutional heritage rebels at the thought of giving government the power to control men's minds."[41]

While the *Miller* test failed to end the controversy over the definition of obscenity and has pleased few free speech advocates with its abandonment of *Roth's* "utterly without redeeming social value" standard, it has emphasized the narrowness of the so-called "obscenity" exception to the First Amendment. When both the audience and the participants, if any, are consenting adults, the First Amendment protects all expression other than that meeting the *Miller* definition of obscenity. And the determination of whether specific expression fits within that definition requires that the state specifically define the conduct or expression to be prohibited; that the expression offend the standards of the local or, at most, state community; and that the literary, artistic, political, or scientific value be judged according to a national, reasonable person standard. Expression not meeting the *Miller* definition, judged according to these procedural and substantive safeguards, is not obscene and is protected by the First Amendment. Such words and phrases as "pornography" or "lewd, lascivious, and filthy" or "XXX," which may be used to describe sexually explicit expression, have no legal significance. Expression that meets the *Miller* definition for obscenity may be prohibited only insofar as the regulation applies to distribution or public display. Under *Stanley*, the mere possession of obscenity is fully protected by the First Amendment.

Miller has largely defined state obscenity law. Rather than merely mark the contours of acceptable obscenity regulation, as the Court anticipated, the case has been followed by virtually all states as articulating the definition of obscenity. Indiana state law, for example, defines obscenity as follows:

> A matter or performance is obscene for purposes of this article if:
>
> (1) The average person, applying contemporary community standards, finds that the dominant theme of the matter or performance, taken as a whole, appeals to the prurient interest in sex;
>
> (2) The matter or performance depicts or describes, in a patently offensive way, sexual conduct; and

(3) The matter or performance, taken as a whole, lacks serious literary, artistic, political, or scientific value.[42]

State law does not define "prurient interest in sex" or "serious literary, artistic, political, or scientific value."

Indiana state law prohibits the knowing or intentional importation, distribution, exhibition, or performance of obscene material:

A person who knowingly or intentionally:

(1) Sends or brings into Indiana obscene matter for sale or distribution; or

(2) Offers to distribute, distributes, or exhibits to another person obscene matter;

commits a Class A misdemeanor. However, the offense is a Class D felony if the obscene matter depicts or describes sexual conduct involving any person who is or appears to be under sixteen (16) years of age.

A person who knowingly or intentionally engages in, participates in, manages, produces, sponsors, presents, exhibits, photographs, films, or videotapes any obscene performance commits a Class A misdemeanor. However, the offense is a Class D felony if the obscene performance depicts or describes sexual conduct involving any person who is or appears to be under sixteen (16) years of age.[43]

Read together, *Miller* and *Stanley* indicate that it is only the threat of possible harm posed by distribution or public performance of obscene material, and not posed by its possession, that permits the criminalization of the former but not the latter. The Court's logic therefore suggests that if it were possible to receive obscenity in the home without posing any of the risks that distribution or public performance were feared inherently to impose — for example, exposure to minors, accidental exposure to unwitting adults, and such "secondary" effects as prostitution and neighborhood deterioration — then the First Amendment would require that the government permit it.[44] In fact, the Court went out of its way in *Stanley* to note that even if it could be shown "that exposure to obscene materials may lead to deviant sexual behavior or crimes of sexual violence" — an assertion for which the Court found "little empirical basis" — "the State may no more prohibit mere possession of obscene matter on the ground that it may lead to anti-social conduct than it may prohibit possession of chemistry books on the ground that they may lead to the manufacture of homemade spirits."[45]

In practice, state law enforcement officials exploit the subjective nature of the first two parts of the *Miller* test, the high cost of litigation, and the political visibility of anti-porn "crackdowns" to effectively threaten many distributors of sexually explicit images and videos. (Suits for text-based obscenity alone are rare.) Defendants often settle rather than endure the tactics of government officials, the cost of a trial, the negative publicity associated with being tried and arrested, and the risk of a conviction. Nonetheless, it is still clear that the law protects a very broad range of sexually explicit expression.

Material that Is Harmful to Minors and Variable Obscenity

When the audience or participants are not limited to consenting adults, courts have interpreted the First Amendment to permit greater regulation, or even prohibition, of sexually explicit expression. This is particularly true when children are involved. For example, the Supreme Court has found that states not only may criminalize the depiction of children in sexually explicit films and photographs, they also may prohibit the distribution and even the mere possession of those films and photographs in an effort to eliminate the market for child pornography.[46]

The government also may constitutionally require suppliers of sexually explicit expression to restrict children's access to that expression. Sometimes referred to as "variable obscenity," this concept permits states to require sellers of non-obscene, "adult" books, magazines, and videos to stock those items in a section of the store inaccessible to children, to display them with opaque wrappers, or to require proof of age from people entering "adult" book and video stores.[47] Indiana, for example, typical of many states, designates some material or performances as "harmful to minors" if:

> 1) It describes or represents, in any form, nudity, sexual conduct, sexual excitement, or sado-masochistic abuse;
>
> 2) Considered as a whole, it appeals to the prurient interest in sex of minors;
>
> 3) It is patently offensive to prevailing standards in the adult community as a whole with respect to what is suitable matter for or performance before minors; and
>
> 4) Considered as a whole, it lacks serious literary, artistic, political, or scientific value for minors.[48]

State law broadly prohibits making such material or performances available to minors.

> A person who knowingly or intentionally:
>
> 1) Disseminates matter to minors that is harmful to minors;
>
> 2) Displays matter that is harmful to minors in an area to which minors have visual, auditory, or physical access, unless each minor is accompanied by his parent or guardian;
>
> 3) Sells or displays for sale to any person matter that is harmful to minors within five hundred feet (500') of the nearest property line of a school or church;
>
> 4) Engages in or conducts a performance before minors that is harmful to minors;
>
> 5) Engages in or conducts a performance that is harmful to minors in an area to which minors have visual, auditory, or physical access, unless each minor is accompanied by his parent or guardian; . . .
>
> commits a Class D felony.[49]

Laws such as this recognize that material that is not obscene for adults nonetheless may be harmful to children. Interestingly, neither legislatures nor courts have sought to identify precisely the risk such material poses to children. Because protecting children is a compelling state interest, courts simply have deferred to legislative determinations that accessing sexually explicit material does in fact harm children. Legislators, in turn, have largely assumed that such harm exists. It is beyond the purview of this book to debate the existence of such harm, but it is sufficient to note that legislatures and courts alike have based a great deal of jurisprudence on the *assumption* that exposure to sexually explicit material does harm children. And courts have therefore permitted extensive regulation of children's access to sexually explicit material. The constitutional limit on those restrictions, according to the Supreme Court, is that they must not limit what adults may read to "only what is fit for children."[50] "Regardless of the strength of the government's interest" in protecting children, the Court has written, "the level of discourse reaching the mailbox simply cannot be limited to that which would be suitable for a sandbox."[51] The Court's most recent cases indicate that no incursion into the First Amendment rights of adults is permissible in order to protect children if it is not necessary and effective as a means of controlling minors' access.[52]

Children, Technology, and Indecency

In most media, it is possible to restrict access by children to sexually explicit expression without also foreclosing access by adults. However, the broadcasting medium has always been thought to present two special problems and therefore has been subject to broader regulation than print media. The Supreme Court first identified these unique features of the broadcast medium in 1978 in *Federal Communications Commission* v. *Pacifica Foundation*.[53] The case involved comedian George Carlin's monologue about the "seven dirty words" broadcast by a New York radio station at 2:00 p.m. on a Tuesday afternoon. A Florida man, who was driving through New York with his 12-year-old son, complained about the broadcast to the Federal Communications Commission (FCC), which exercises exclusive authority over broadcasting and interstate telephone communications in the United States. (The regulation of most other media, by contrast, takes place at the state level.) The FCC asserted that broadcasting the Carlin monologue in the afternoon could subject the radio station to administrative penalties, though the commission declined to impose any penalties in this case. Pacifica Corporation, owner of the New York station, sued the FCC, claiming that even the potential of a sanction violated the First Amendment.

The Supreme Court upheld the commission's position on the ground that the broadcasting medium is different from print when evaluating regulations designed to protect children. First, the Court noted, "broadcasting is uniquely accessible to children, even those too young to read. Although Cohen's written message ["Fuck the draft"] might have been incomprehensible to a first grader, Pacifica's broadcast could have enlarged a child's vocabulary in an instant."[54] Second, because it has offered comparatively few programming choices, broadcasting traditionally has involved children and adults in the same audience. As Justice Powell wrote, concurring in *Pacifica,* "[s]ellers of printed and recorded matter and exhibitors of motion pictures and live performances may be required to shut their doors to children, but such a requirement has no effect on adults' access."[55] Adults can continue to read "adult" literature and view "adult" films; the exclusion of children from such content in no way hinders the access of adults.

As a result of these technological differences, the FCC, Congress, and the courts have created a definition for a new category of sexually explicit expression — "indecency." According to that definition, broadcast programs are indecent if they contain "language or material that depicts or describes in terms patently offensive as measured by contemporary standards for the broadcast medium, sexual or excretory activities or organs."[56] Because there is no effective way to determine the age of members of the audience watching broadcast television programs — the situation is technologically different for cable television — and because the images and sounds included in television broadcasts are accessible even to children too young to read, Congress and the FCC have "channeled" the airing of indecent material to nighttime when, they have assumed, fewer viewers are unsupervised children.

The Supreme Court reviews regulations designed to protect children from sexually explicit television programming under a more lenient standard of scrutiny than the Court applies to regulations applicable to print media. Despite that greater leeway, however, the FCC has experienced considerable difficulty in crafting indecency regulations that pass even modest First Amendment review by the Court. The commission worked for almost a decade before finally promulgating indecency rules that are constitutional. In 1987 the FCC proposed sanctioning broadcasters who aired indecent programming before midnight; after midnight, the commission concluded, it is reasonable to expect that the risk of unsupervised children in the audience is minimized and therefore proposed permitting indecent programming to be broadcast without fear of liability.[57] The following year, the Court of Appeals for the District of Columbia vacated the commission's post-midnight safe harbor as unsupported by evidence and unnecessarily intrusive on adults' First Amendment rights.[58] Two months after the court's decision, Congress instructed the commission to promulgate regulations enforcing the prohibition on indecency on a 24-hour-a-day basis.[59] The commission complied by issuing a regulation banning all broadcasts of indecent material.[60]

The following year, the Court of Appeals remanded a challenge to the FCC's new rules to enable the commission to solicit more information relevant to the congressionally mandated 24-hour ban.[61] The commission reported its conclusions in *In re Enforcement of Prohibitions Against Broadcast Indecency in 18 U.S.C. § 1464.*[62] In that report, the FCC found that the compelling government interest in protecting "children ages 17 and under" from indecent broadcasts would not be promoted effectively by any means more narrowly tailored than a 24-hour prohibition. The appellate court disagreed and struck down the total ban on indecent broadcasts.[63] Congress again intervened, passing the Public Telecommunications Act of 1992, which required the commission to promulgate regulations to prohibit the broadcasting of indecent programming 1) between 6 a.m. and 10 p.m. by any public radio or television station that goes off the air at or before midnight and 2) between 6 a.m. and midnight by any other radio or television station.[64] The commission complied and issued the required rules,[65] which the Court of Appeals initially overturned,[66] but then upheld, after modifying the safe harbor to 10:00 p.m. to 6:00 a.m. for all broadcasters.[67]

Outside of the context of over-the-air broadcasting, which the Court has found warrants less First Amendment protection because of its technological features, the Supreme Court evaluates the constitutionality of regulations on indecency under "strict scrutiny" — the Court's highest standard of constitutional review.[68] Under strict scrutiny, "the State must show that its regulation is necessary to serve a compelling state interest and is narrowly drawn to achieve that end."[69] In *Sable Communications of California, Inc. v. Federal Communications Commission*,[70] the Court addressed the interaction between technology and the presence of children in the audience with regard to sexually explicit telephone services. The case arose when, after a decade of experimenting with various regulatory measures designed to restrict access by children to so-called dial-a-porn services, Congress passed a law prohibiting the transmission of obscene and indecent expression for commercial purposes.[71] The Supreme Court responded with a stinging rebuke, unanimously invalidating the law as it applied to indecent communications. "Sexual expression which is indecent but not obscene is protected by the First Amendment."[72] The Court found that for the government to regulate indecent expression it must do so not only in furtherance of a "compelling" state interest, but also "by narrowly drawn regulations designed to serve those interests without unnecessarily interfering with First Amendment freedoms."[73] This is the highest form of scrutiny applied by the Court to any regulation of expression. The fact that the expression was sexually explicit and commercial was irrelevant.[74]

Communications Decency Act

The Internet poses the newest challenge to regulators concerned with protecting children from sexually explicit expression. In June 1995 the Senate passed the Communications Decency Act (CDA) as an amendment to the Telecommunications Competition and

Deregulation Act of 1996. As passed by the Senate, the CDA would have criminalized the transmission of "any indecent communication" by means of "any telecommunications device" to any person under 18 years of age (as well as the transmission of obscenity to any person, which current law already prohibits), or knowingly permitting any "telecommunications facility" under one's control to be used to make or make available any indecent communication to any person under 18 years of age.[75]

The Conference Committee charged with reconciling the House and Senate versions of the larger telecommunications reform act subsequently amended the CDA to criminalize only the use of an "interactive computer system" to send or display to a minor "any comment, request, suggestion, proposal, image, or other communication that, in context, depicts or describes, in terms patently offensive as measured by contemporary community standards, sexual or excretory activities or organs."[76] Although this phrase does not match either the Supreme Court's definition of obscenity in *Miller* or the FCC's definition of indecency, the conference committee's report indicated that the phrase is intended to "codif[y] the definition of indecency" from *Pacifica* and have the "same meaning as established" in *Pacifica* and *Sable*.[77] The penalties for transmitting or displaying an offending communication to a minor included a fine of up to $250,000 and/or imprisonment for as long as two years.

The Act extended liability to anyone who knowingly sends or displays the offending communication to a minor, and to anyone who knowingly permits a telecommunications facility under his or her control to be used for such an activity, irrespective of whether "the user of such service placed the call or initiated the communication."[78] This broad liability provision was subject to exceptions for people 1) whose sole involvement with the offending communication consists of "providing access or connection to or from a facility, system, or network not under that person's control"; 2) who have taken "in good faith, reasonable, effective, and appropriate actions under the circumstances to restrict or prevent access by minors to a communication specified" in this section; or 3) who have "restricted access to such communication by requiring use of a verified credit card, debit account, adult access code, or adult personal identification number."[79]

The first of these exemptions on its face offered little protection, because few service providers, other than perhaps telephone companies, provide access or a connection without also exercising some control over content. The application of the second exemption depended entirely on the meaning of "reasonable, effective, and appropriate." It is virtually impossible for an information provider, as opposed to a user, to effectively prohibit access by minors. If warnings are ignored, and if parents do not control their children's use of the Internet or avail themselves of technological devices that control use, the service provider is powerless to restrict access by minors. However, the conference committee report provided that the "word 'effective' is given its common meaning and does not require an absolute 100% restriction of access to be judged effective."[80] Even with this qualification, the Act raised the specter of the government prosecuting parents who allow their adolescent children to watch a television program containing sexually explicit material.

The third exemption — for those who have "restricted access to such communication by requiring use of a verified credit card, debit account, adult access code, or adult personal identification number" — threatened to alter substantially the character of the Internet. The Internet today is characterized by unimpeded, anonymous provision of, and access to, information. The third defense would have required that service providers verify the identity and age of users. Even then, it would not protect information suppliers who post material to a newsgroup or other site that has no gatekeeping mechanism.

The conference committee reported out the CDA as part of the Telecommunications Competition and Deregulation Act of 1996 on 31 January 1996. Although there had been no public hearings and no opportunity for public comment on the amended text, the House of Representatives waived its standing rule giving Members at least three days to review conference reports.[81] The House

53

then passed the Act on 1 February 1996, voting 414 to 16.[82] The Senate also passed the Act on the same day, voting 91 to 5.[83]

President Clinton signed the bill into law on 8 February 1996. That same day, critics of the CDA, led by the American Civil Liberties Union, filed a lawsuit challenging the Act's constitutionality. One week later, the U.S. District Court for the Eastern District of Pennsylvania issued a temporary restraining order against enforcement of the Act, on the basis that the Act was unconstitutionally vague.[84] A broader consortium of 37 organizations, including the American Library Association and Microsoft, filed a second, similar suit on February 26.

On 11 June 1996 a three-judge panel of the U.S. District Court for the Eastern District of Pennsylvania voted unanimously to grant a preliminary injunction against enforcement of the CDA, based on their belief that the Act was unconstitutionally broad and vague.[85] In a sweeping opinion, the judges surveyed the history and characteristics of the Internet, finding that "[f]our related characteristics of Internet communication have a transcendent importance to our shared holding that the CDA is unconstitutional on its face" and distinguish the medium from broadcasting:

> First, the Internet presents very low barriers to entry. Second, these barriers to entry are identical for both speakers and listeners. Third, as a result of those low barriers, astoundingly diverse content is available on the Internet. Fourth, the Internet provides significant access to all who wish to speak in the medium and even creates a relative parity among speakers.[86]

These features led at least one of the three judges to conclude that "Congress may not regulate indecency on the Internet *at all*."[87]

The court then rejected each of the government's arguments in support of the statute's constitutionality. The outcome at the District Court level surprised few observers, but the scope of the decision and the total repudiation of the government's position surprised many.

The government appealed the District Court's decision to the U.S. Supreme Court, which issued its opinion on 26 June 1997.[88]

In a 7-2 decision, the Court struck down the law as overbroad and vague, at least matching, if not exceeding, the breadth of the District Court's opinion. Even the two dissenters, Chief Justice Rehnquist and Justice O'Connor, agreed that portions of the CDA were unconstitutional on their face.

The Court's analysis is significant because it suggests the considerable difficulties facing future restrictions on Internet content. Justice Stevens began his opinion for the Court by quoting approvingly from the District Court's opinion about the novelty and distinctiveness of the Internet. "The Internet is 'a unique and wholly new medium of worldwide human communication,'" he noted. "It is 'no exaggeration to conclude that the content on the Internet is as diverse as human thought.'" Most significantly, "'[n]o single organization controls any membership in the Web, nor is there any centralized point from which individual Web sites or services can be blocked from the Web.'" "'Once a provider posts its content on the Internet, it cannot prevent that content from entering any community.'" These conclusions by the Court are critical, because they created the factual basis on which the Court could distinguish the Internet from broadcast television and radio, which are subject to lower First Amendment scrutiny.

The Court then outlined the legal basis for distinguishing its prior broadcasting and telephone cases. The Court determined that the Internet was not subject to the same history of regulation that had applied to broadcasting: "Neither before nor after the enactment of the CDA have the vast democratic fora of the Internet been subject to the type of government supervision and regulation that has attended the broadcast industry." Nor is the Internet a scare or invasive medium, as the Court has characterized broadcasting.

Having concluded that there was "no basis for qualifying the level of First Amendment scrutiny" that should be applied to the Internet, the Court then proceeded to apply its traditional First Amendment jurisprudence to find that the Act did not meet the high level of First Amendment scrutiny required of a direct, content-based regulation of constitutionally protected expression. In particular, the Court found that it was either impossible or potentially very costly for Internet content providers to ascertain and comply with the requirements of the CDA. Rather than impose a constitutionally minimal interference with adult access in order to protect children, the Court found that the Act was "vague," "ineffective," and certain to impose "significant burdens," particularly on noncommercial service providers. "The breadth of this content-based restriction of speech imposes an especially heavy burden on the Government to explain why a less restrictive provision would not be as effective as the CDA. It has not done so." Justice Stevens concluded for the Court:

> We agree with the District Court's conclusion that the CDA places an unacceptably heavy burden on protected speech, and that the defenses do not constitute the sort of "narrow tailoring" that will save an otherwise patently invalid unconstitutional provision. In Sable, we remarked that the speech restriction at issue there amounted to "burning the house to roast the pig." The CDA, casting a far darker shadow over free speech, threatens to torch a large segment of the Internet community.[89]

The extraordinary protection of the First Amendment restricts government efforts to regulate the content not only of print media, but also of television and radio broadcasting and of the Internet. However, that protection is not absolute. The distribution and performance or display of obscenity may constitutionally be regulated in all three media. And the government may require content providers and distributors to take steps to restrict children's access to sexually explicit material that may be harmful for minors, while not obscene for adults. The limit on such variable obscenity statutes is that they may not unnecessarily restrict adults' access to the expression at issue.

Only the broadcast medium is subject to different First Amendment scrutiny. According to the Supreme Court, that difference is the result of the unique accessibility of broadcast content to children and the difficulty of separating children from adults in the audience for broadcasting. As a result of these two characteristics of the broadcast medium, broadcasters may be required to channel their sexually explicit expression to decrease the likelihood of children being exposed to it and to increase the opportunities for parents to oversee their children's television viewing. Regulations on broadcast indecency must not, however, interfere unnecessarily with adult access. And, after the Supreme Court's decision in *Reno* v. *American Civil Liberties Union,* it is now clear that the lower First Amendment scrutiny applicable to broadcasting is not appropriate for the Internet. The Internet stands shoulder to shoulder with print media in the full protection of the First Amendment. The next chapter examines the regulation of sexually explicit expression on the Internet.

Notes

1. NAACP v. Claiborne Hardware Company, 458 U.S. 886, 913 (1982); *see also* Mills v. Alabama, 384 U.S. 214, 218-19 (1966) ("Whatever differences may exist about interpretations of the First Amendment, there is practically universal agreement that a major purpose of that Amendment was to protect the free discussion of governmental affairs."); Roth v. United States, 354 U.S. 476, 484 (1957) (The First Amendment was "fashioned to assure the unfettered interchange of ideas for the bringing about of political and social changes desired by the people."); Stromberg v. California, 283 U.S. 359, 369 (1931) ("The maintenance of the opportunity for free political discussion to the end that government may be responsive to the will of the people and that changes may be obtained by lawful means, an opportunity essential to the security of the Republic, is a fundamental principle of our constitutional system.").
2. Robert Bork, "Neutral Principles and Some First Amendment Problems," *Indiana Law Journal* 47 (1971): 1, 23.
3. New York Times Company v. Sullivan, 376 U.S. 254, 269 (1964).
4. Gertz v. Robert Welch, Inc., 418 U.S. 323, 339-340 (1974).
5. Martin Redish, "Product Health Claims and the First Amendment: Scientific Expression and the Twilight Zone of Commercial Speech," *Vanderbilt Law Review* 43 (1990): 1433, 1435.
6. Oliver Wendell Holmes, "The Path of the Law," *Harvard Law Review* 10 (1897): 447, 466.
7. Texas v. Johnson, 491 U.S. 397, 414 (1989).

8. Rodney A. Smolla, *Free Speech in an Open Society* (New York: Alfred A. Knopf, 1992), p. 46. *See also* Hustler Magazine, Inc. v. Falwell, 485 U.S. 46, 55-56 (1988); City Council of Los Angeles v. Taxpayers for Vincent, 466 U.S. 789, 804 (1984).

9. Gertz v. Robert Welch, Inc., 418 U.S. 323, 339-340 (1974).

10. *See* Cohen v. California, 403 U.S. 15 (1971); *Hustler,* 485 U.S. 46.

11. 337 U.S. 1, 4 (1949).

12. 394 U.S. 557, 566 (1969), quoting Kingsley International Pictures Corp. v. Regents, 360 U.S. 684, 688 (1959).

13. David A.J. Richards, "Free Speech and Obscenity Law: Toward a Moral Theory of the First Amendment," *University of Pennsylvania Law Review* 123 (1974): 45, 62.

14. Thomas Emerson, *The System of Freedom of Expression* (New York: Random House, 1970), p. 6.

15. 274 U.S. 357, 375 (1927) (Brandeis, J., concurring).

16. Smolla, *op. cit.*, pp. 10-11 (emphasis in original).

17. 403 U.S. 15, 25 (1971).

18. 376 U.S. 254, 271-72 (1964) [quoting NAACP v. Button, 371 U.S. 415, 433 (1963)].

19. R.A.V. v. City of St. Paul, Minnesota, 505 U.S. 377 (1992); New York Times Company v. United States, 403 U.S. 713 (1971). *See generally,* Fred H. Cate, "The First Amendment and the National Information Infrastructure," *Wake Forest Law Review* 30 (1995): 1, 10-11.

20. R.A.V., 505 U.S. 377; Texas v. Johnson, 491 U.S. 397 (1989); Consolidated Edison Company v. Public Service Commission, 447 U.S. 530 (1980); Wooley v. Maynard, 430 U.S. 705 (1977); Miami Herald Publishing Company v. Tornillo, 418 U.S. 241, 244 (1974); West Virginia State Board of Education v. Barnette, 319 U.S. 624. *See generally*, Cate, "The First Amendment and the National Information Infrastructure," pp. 11-14.

21. Joseph Burstyn, Inc. v. Wilson, 343 U.S. 495 (1952).

22. Philadelphia Newspapers, Inc. v. Hepps, 475 U.S. 767 (1986); Gertz v. Robert Welch, Inc., 418 U.S. 323 (1974); *New York Times,* 376 U.S. 254. *See generally,* Cate, *op. cit.*, pp. 14-16.

23. United States v. Eichman, 496 U.S. 310 (1990); Texas v. Johnson, 491 U.S. 397 (1989). *See generally,* Cate, *op. cit.*, p. 16.

24. Minneapolis Star & Tribune Company v. Minnesota Commissioner of Revenue, 460 U.S. 575 (1983); First National Bank v. Bellotti,

435 U.S. 765 (1978); Buckley v. Valeo, 424 U.S. 1 (1976). *See generally,* Cate, *op. cit.,* pp. 16-18.

25. Smith v. California, 361 U.S. 147, 152-53 (1959).
26. Id., p. 153.
27. Id., pp. 153-54.
28. 354 U.S. 476, 485 (1957).
29. Jacobellis v. Ohio, 378 U.S. 184, 197 (1964) (Stewart, J., concurring).
30. Robert Corn-Revere, "New Age Comstockery," *CommLaw Conspectus* 4 (1996): 173.
31. Paris Adult Theater v. Slayton, 413 U.S. 49, 92-93 (1973) (Brennan, J., dissenting).
32. Memoirs v. Massachusetts, 383 U.S. 413 (1966) (emphasis in original).
33. 413 U.S. 15, 24 (1973).
34. Brockett v. Spokane Arcades, Inc., 472 U.S. 491, 498 (1985).
35. 413 U.S. 20.
36. Id., pp. 30-33.
37. Pope v. Illinois, 481 U.S. 497 (1987).
38. 394 U.S. 557 (1969).
39. Id., p. 568.
40. Id., p. 564.
41. Id., p. 565.
42. Burns Indiana Code Annotated § 35-49-2-1 (1996).
43. Id § 35-49-3-2.
44. 394 U.S. 566-68.
45. Id., pp. 566-67.
46. New York v. Ferber, 458 U.S. 747 (1982).
47. Ginsberg v. New York, 390 U.S. 629 (1968); American Booksellers v. Webb, 919 F.2d 1493 (11th Cir. 1990); Upper Midwest Booksellers Association v. Minneapolis, 780 F.2d 1389 (8th Cir. 1985).
48. Burns Indiana Code Annotated § 35-49-2-2 (1995).
49. Id. § 35-49-3-3.
50. Butler v. Michigan, 352 U.S. 380, 383 (1957).
51. Bolger v. Youngs Drug Products Corp., 463 U.S. 60, 74-75 (1983).
52. Denver Area Educational Telecommunications Consortium, Inc. v. Federal Communications Commission, _ U.S. _, 116 S. Ct. 2374 (1996); Sable Communications of California, Inc. v. Federal Communications Commission, 492 U.S. 115 (1989).

53. 438 U.S. 726 (1978).
54. Id., p. 749.
55. Id., p. 758 (Powell, J., concurring in part).
56. New Indecency Enforcement Standards to be Applied to All Broadcast and Amateur Radio Licensees, FCC No. 87-153, 62 Rad. Reg. 2d (P&F) 1218 (1987) (public notice).
57. In re Infinity Broadcasting Corp. of Penn., 3 F.C.C.R. 930, 937 n. 47 (1987).
58. Action for Children's Television v. Federal Communications Commission, 852 F.2d 1332 (D.C. Cir. 1988).
59. Pub. L. No. 100-459, § 608, 102 Stat. 2186, 2228 (1988).
60. Enforcement of Prohibitions Against Broadcast Obscenity and Indecency, in 18 U.S.C. § 1464, 4 FCC Rcd. 457 (1988).
61. Action for Children's Television v. Federal Communications Commission, No. 88-1916 (D.C. Cir. 13 September 1989).
62. 5 F.C.C.R. 5297 (1990).
63. Action for Children's Television v. Federal Communications Commission, 932 F.2d 1504 (D.C. Cir. 1991), *cert denied,* 503 U.S. 913 (1992).
64. Pub. L. No. 102-356 § 16(a), 106 Stat. 949 (1992).
65. 1993 Report and Order, 8 F.C.C.R. p. 711; 47 C.F.R. § 73.3999 (1994).
66. Action for Children's Television v. Federal Communications Commission, 11 F.3d 170 (D.C. Cir. 1994) (per curiam).
67. Action for Children's Television v. Federal Communications Commission, 58 F.3d 654 (D.C. Cir. 1995) (en banc), *cert. denied,* Pacifica Foundation v. Federal Communications Commission, __ U.S. __, 116 S. Ct. 701 (1996).
68. The Supreme Court has justified applying a lower standard of First Amendment scrutiny to regulations affecting radio and television broadcasting based on a variety of rationales, the most prominent of which is the scarcity of the electromagnetic spectrum that broadcasting requires. In *Red Lion Broadcasting Company* v. *Federal Communications Commission,* the unanimous Court reasoned: "Where there are substantially more individuals who want to broadcast than there are frequencies to allocate, it is idle to posit an unbridgeable First Amendment right to broadcast comparable to the right of every individual to speak, write, or publish." 395 U.S. 367, 388 (1969). Because of scarcity, Justice White wrote for the Court,

"the Government is permitted to put restraints on licensees. . . . It is the right of the viewers and listeners, not the right of the broadcasters, which is paramount." Id., p. 391 (citations omitted).

The concept of scarcity has been under attack for more than a decade. Critics question whether there was ever any more scarcity in the case of broadcasting than there was in print media, whether the government created whatever scarcity existed, whether scarcity is inherently bad because it is essential to the operation of a market, and, even if scarcity does exist and is harmful, whether it served as a logical foundation for the many regulations that the government has derived from it, not merely licensing, but also character and fitness qualifications for broadcasters, obligations to air programming covering matters of public interest, obligations to give or sell time to persons attacked in broadcasts and to candidates for public office, and obligations to air children's programming, avoid indecency, not advertise cigarettes or lotteries, and hundreds of additional requirements. *See* Cate, "The First Amendment and the National Information Infrastructure," pp. 37-40.

69. Arkansas Writers' Project, Inc. v. Ragland, 481 U.S. 221, 231 (1987).

70. 492 U.S. 115 (1989).

71. Congress began its effort to regulate "dial-a-porn" in 1983, when it passed the Federal Communications Commission Authorization Act, Pub. L. 98-214, § 8(b), 97 Stat. 1470, which made it a crime to use telephone facilities to make "obscene or indecent" interstate telephone communications "for commercial purposes to any person under eighteen years of age or to any other person without that person's consent." 47 U.S.C. § 223(b)(1)(A) (1982 Supp. V). The statute required the FCC to promulgate regulations laying out the means by which dial-a-porn sponsors could screen out underage callers. Id. § 223(b)(2). The FCC initially promulgated regulations that would have established a defense to message providers operating only between the hours of 9 p.m. and 8 a.m. and to providers requiring payment by credit card before transmission of the dial-a-porn message. Restrictions on Obscene or Indecent Telephone Message Services, codified at 47 C.F.R. § 64.201 (1988).

In *Carlin Communications, Inc.* v. *Federal Communications Commission,* 749 F.2d 113 (2d Cir. 1984), the Court of Appeals for the Second Circuit rejected and remanded the commission's rules.

61

In 1985 the FCC promulgated new regulations that continued to permit credit card payment as a defense to prosecution, while adding a defense based on use of access codes. Enforcement of Prohibitions Against the Use of Common Carriers for the Transmission of Obscene Materials, 50 Fed. Reg. 42,699, 42,705 (1985) (FCC, final rule). The FCC rejected a proposal for "exchange blocking," which would block or screen telephone numbers at the customer's premises or at the telephone company offices. In *Carlin Communications, Inc.* v. *Federal Communications Commission,* 787 F.2d 846 (2d Cir. 1986), the Court of Appeals set aside the new regulations because of the FCC's failure adequately to consider customer premises blocking. The FCC then promulgated a third set of regulations, which again rejected customer premises blocking but added to the prior defenses of credit card payments and access codes the defense of message scrambling. Enforcement of Prohibitions Against the Use of Common Carriers for the Transmission of Obscene Materials, 52 Fed. Reg. 17,760 (1987) (FCC, third report and order).

In 1988, in *Carlin Communications, Inc.* v. *Federal Communications Commission,* 837 F.2d 546 (2d Cir.), *cert. denied,* 488 U.S. 924 (1988), the Court of Appeals for the Second Circuit invalidated § 223(b) as it applied to non-obscene speech, *id.,* at 560, 561, and remanded the case to the commission to determine whether a less restrictive technological means was available for controlling access by minors to obscene expression. In April 1988, Congress responded by amending section 223(b) of the Communications Act to prohibit outright indecent as well as obscene interstate commercial telephone communications directed to any person regardless of age. Child Protection and Obscenity Enforcement Act of 1988, Pub. L. No. 100-297, 102 Stat. 424.(amending 47 U.S.C. § 223(b) to prohibit obscene and indecent telephone calls).

72. 492 U.S. 126.

73. Id., p. 128 (citations omitted) [quoting Schaumberg v. Citizens for a Better Environment, 444 U.S. 620, 637 (1980)].

74. Until 1976 the Supreme Court declined to extend First Amendment protection to "commercial speech." In *Virginia State Board of Pharmacy* v. *Virginia Citizens Consumer Council, Inc.,* 425 U.S. 748, 762 (1976), the Supreme Court emphasized the importance of commercial information, in this case information on pharmaceutical prices, for intelligent consumer decision-making and held that such

speech was protected by the First Amendment. The Court noted, however, that the "greater objectivity and hardiness" of commercial speech warranted a lesser standard of protection than for other forms of expression. Id., p. 772. Four years later, in *Central Hudson Gas and Electric Corporation* v. *Public Service Commission,* 447 U.S. 557 (1980), the Court set forth a four-part test for determining exactly what that standard of protection should be: 1) the speech must concern a lawful activity and not be misleading; 2) the government must assert a substantial interest for its regulation; 3) the regulation must directly advance that interest; and 4) the regulation must be no more extensive than necessary to serve the government interest. *Id.* at 566. In 1989 the Court altered the fourth prong to require that the regulation merely be "narrowly tailored" to serve the governmental interest. Board of Trustees v. Fox, 492 U.S. 469 (1989).

75. Telecommunications Competition and Deregulation Act of 1996, S. 652, 104th Cong., 2nd Sess. § 402(a).
76. Id. § 502(e).
77. H R. CONF. REP. No. 458, 104th Cong., 2nd Sess. (1996).
78. Id., § 502(d).
79. Id. § 502(e) (5).
80. Id.
81. H.R. RES.353, 104th Cong., 2nd Sess., 142 CONG. REC. H1145 (1996).
82. 142 CONG. REC. D56-01 (daily ed. 1 Feb. 1996).
83. 142 CONG. REC. D54-02 (daily ed. 1 Feb. 1996).
84. American Civil Liberties Union v. Reno, Civ. Action No. 96-963 (E.D. Pa. Feb. 15, 1996) (temporary restraining order).
85. American Civil Liberties Union v. Reno, 929 F. Supp. 824 (E.D. Pa. 1996), *aff'd,* _ U.S. _, 1997 U.S. LEXIS 4037 (1997).
86. Id., p. 877 (Dalzell, J., concurring).
87. Id. (emphasis added).
88. Reno v. American Civil Liberties Union, _ U.S. _, 1997 U.S. LEXIS 4037 (1997).
89. Id., 1997 U.S. LEXIS 4037, *67 (citation omitted).

CHAPTER FOUR

CONTROLLING SEXUALLY EXPLICIT EXPRESSION ON THE INTERNET

In this chapter I take up two important areas with regard to controlling sexually explicit expression on the Internet: legal regulation and technological and other nonregulatory means for controlling access.

Legal Regulation

Obscenity. The distribution or public exhibition of sexually explicit expression that meets the *Miller* definition for obscenity may be banned constitutionally, whether it is printed, broadcast, mailed, distributed by telephone, or made available via the Internet.[1] If that sexually explicit expression depicts children, the government may constitutionally criminalize its creation, dissemination, and, in this limited context, even its possession.

As a practical matter, liability for Internet obscenity presents few issues for teachers, librarians, and school administrators, because these professionals are unlikely to be downloading material meeting the stringent test for obscenity any more than they are likely to bring obscene books or movies into the school. Moreover, law enforcement officials traditionally have prosecuted the people and organizations who create and distribute obscene material, rather than the users who access it. This seems likely to remain the case with Internet-based obscenity.

However, irrespective of the medium, knowingly downloading or otherwise bringing obscene material into the classroom would violate state law in every U.S. jurisdiction. On the other hand, the failure of teachers or librarians to prevent students from accessing such material would almost certainly not violate obscenity laws, especially if those professionals were unaware of the content that students were accessing. However, the failure to supervise students' access to obscene expression is likely to violate professional standards and administrative polices of education organizations, as well as to provoke public outcry.

The medium is not irrelevant to the regulation of obscenity, because it affects both the application of the *Miller* test and the range of liable parties. The relationship between obscenity law and the technological medium of communication is shown clearly in the recent criminal prosecution of Robert and Carleen Thomas. The Thomases were convicted by a Memphis, Tennessee, jury in 1994 for operating the Amateur Action electronic bulletin board in Milpitas, California.[2] Amateur Action provided a wide variety of sexually explicit pictures to paying subscribers, who connected to the bulletin board using modems and telephone lines. A Tennessee postal inspector joined the Thomas' bulletin board and downloaded sexually explicit images. He also requested that a videotape be sent to him by UPS, and he sent to the Thomases an unsolicited videotape of child pornography. The Memphis jury acquitted the Thomases on charges of purveying child pornography, but convicted them on 11 counts of interstate transmission and transportation of obscenity. Judge Julia Gibbons sentenced Robert and Carleen Thomas to 37 and 30 months in prison, respectively, and authorized the government to seize the Amateur Action computers.[3]

On appeal before the U.S. Court of Appeals for the Sixth Circuit, three of the principal issues were whether it was constitutional for a Memphis jury to apply Memphis standards when evaluating whether the material downloaded from Milpitas, California, met the *Miller* definition of "obscenity," whether the Thomases should be liable for an action — downloading the material — that was performed by somebody else, and how "community" should be defined in cyberspace. In its amicus brief, the Electronic Frontier Foundation, a Washington-based, not-for-profit organization that explores legal, policy, and social issues surrounding information technologies, wrote:

> Tennessee is but a single locality that can access the international telecommunications network generally and the Amateur Action bulletin board system specifically. Robert and Carleen Thomas had no physical contacts with the State of Tennessee, they had not advertised in any medium directed primarily at Tennessee, they had not physically visited Tennessee, nor had they any assets or other contacts there. The law enforcement official in Tennessee, not the Thomases, took the actions required to gain access to the materials, and it was his action, not the Thomases, that caused them to be "transported" into Tennessee (such as copies to his local hard disk). The Thomases may indeed have been entirely unaware that they had somehow entered the Tennessee market and had subjected themselves to the standards applicable in that community.[4]

Applying Memphis standards to the Thomases runs contrary to the Supreme Court's position in *Miller,* that "[p]eople in different States vary in their tastes and attitudes, and this diversity is not to be strangled by the absolutism of imposed uniformity."[5] Since the Internet — like the telephone system used to access the Amateur Action bulletin board — crosses all state lines, allowing local juries to use local standards when applying the first two prongs of the *Miller* test necessarily means that Internet content across the nation will be judged by standards embraced by the most conservative communities. Operators of a telephone- or Internet-based bulletin board cannot make their services available to the public while restricting access by people in specific states.

The Thomases' conviction also calls into question who should be liable for violating obscenity laws. There was no evidence that the

Thomases transmitted the electronic images (the videotape shipped by UPS is a different matter); the postal inspector arguably transmitted the images when he downloaded the material.

Finally, the case raises important issues about the meaning of "community" in the Internet context, where traditional notions of geography are no longer relevant. Should the Court abandon the community-based approach it adopted in *Miller* or should it define a new type of community — a virtual community that takes into account the technological realities of the medium?

The U.S. Court of Appeals for the Sixth Circuit ultimately rejected these arguments and upheld the Thomases' conviction.[6] The case nonetheless illustrates the fact that even though obscenity law is applied without regard for the medium of communication, the medium poses important issues about how obscenity will be measured, by whom it will be measured, and against whom the law will be applied. While the Sixth Circuit chose to ignore the significance of those issues in *United States* v. *Thomas,* it remains to be seen how subsequent judicial decisions will deal with them. For the present, however, obscenity law appears likely to be applied to the Internet precisely as it has been applied to other media.

Indecency. The more difficult and more relevant concern for educators and other Internet users is the liability that may result from accessing, or providing access to, sexually explicit but non-obscene expression on the Internet. Given the broad language of variable obscenity statutes in many states, it is possible that resources that a teacher or librarian would find educationally valuable also might fit within the state law's definition of material that is harmful to minors. The District Court in *American Civil Liberties Union* v. *Reno* noted that the Communications Decency Act would have targeted not only commercial pornography, but also valuable, noncommercial information:

> Plaintiff Human Rights Watch, Inc., offers information on its Internet site regarding reported human rights abuses around the world. Plaintiff National Writers Union provides a forum for writers on issues of concern to them. Plaintiff Stop Prisoner Rape, Inc., posts text, graphics, and statistics

regarding the incidence and prevention of rape in prisons. Plaintiff Critical Path AIDS Project, Inc., offers information on safer sex, the transmission of HIV, and the treatment of AIDS.[7]

The court concluded: "[S]ome of the material that plaintiffs post online — such as information regarding protection from AIDS, birth control or prison rape — is sexually explicit and may be considered 'indecent' or 'patently offensive' in some communities."[8]

With the Supreme Court's invalidation of the CDA, the legal risk to educators is quite low. Most state laws define material that is harmful to minors to include only that which "considered as a whole. . . appeals to the prurient interest in sex of minors" and "lacks serious literary, artistic, political, or scientific value for minors."[9] Moreover, these laws usually require that the harmful material be provided "knowingly or intentionally."[10] The failure to control students' access to sexually explicit expression is unlikely to satisfy that requirement. Finally, most state variable obscenity laws provide a specific exemption for teachers and librarians, particularly at public institutions, who act with a legitimate educational purpose. Indiana, for example, provides two relevant defenses:

> (1) That the matter was disseminated or that the performance was performed for legitimate scientific or educational purposes; [or]
> (2) That the matter was disseminated or displayed to or that the performance was performed before the recipient by a bona fide school, museum, or public library that qualifies for certain property tax exemptions under IC 6-1.1-10, or by an employee of such a school, museum, or public library acting within the scope of his employment.[11]

As a result, educators enjoy virtual immunity from laws protecting minors from harmful expression.

Given the history of controversy that has surrounded many schools' and libraries' decisions concerning the materials they acquire, it would seem worthwhile to go beyond the question of liability for online sexually explicit expression and to consider the risk to children in encountering such content on the Internet and the constitutional value of not seeking to purge the Internet of sexually explicit expression. The first issue is addressed below; the second is the subject of the next chapter.

Controlling Access

The likelihood that minors will encounter sexually explicit expression on the Internet is determined primarily by four factors: the characteristics of the medium, the behavior of online information providers, the use of technological filters, and the predilections of minors as informed and overseen by adults.

At first glance, the Internet may appear to present the same issues as broadcast television when it comes to distinguishing between adults and children in the audience. Television and the Internet share visible characteristics: both are transmitted into the home from distant locations and displayed on video screens. Although most Internet traffic today consists of text, a large volume of images, sounds, and even video is available via the Internet. These are every bit as likely to "enlarge a child's vocabulary in an instant"[12] as is broadcast television. Given the unmoderated and immoderate nature of the Internet, that new vocabulary may be startling indeed.

However, there are important technological differences between television and the Internet. For example, it is easier for children to access television than computer networks, bulletin boards, and electronic e-mail. To use the Internet, a series of affirmative, often skilled acts are required, as is demonstrated by the number of "user friendly" articles, books, videotapes, and consulting services directed at helping users unlock the Internet. At minimum, accessing the Internet requires a computer, a modem or network card, a telephone line or other connection, an account number, and a password. To access sexually explicit expression on the Internet requires, in addition to the hardware and account information, a program to connect to the network and a program to browse the material found there. To view images in newsgroups also requires a decoding program and a program to view the decoded images, though today these usually are included with the web browser. Once all of this technology is in place and the know-how is obtained, a user must subscribe to a service, dial into a network or bulletin board, and then select specific material to be accessed.

It is not that children cannot access sexually explicit material on the Internet; rather, it is that networked digital information does not enter the home with the ease of broadcast television. Courts have recognized the significance of this point in the context of cable television, which requires that the user obtain special wiring or other equipment, subscribe to a cable service, and then select from among dozens of channels. As a result of these features, courts have found that cable programming is simply harder to access than broadcast programming and therefore should not be subject to indecency regulations applicable to broadcasting.[13] Internet resources are clearly more difficult to access than either broadcast or cable programming.

In addition, information providers on the Internet take advantage of a greater ability to segregate audience members than do broadcast programmers. The broadcast programmer has no way of controlling who watches a show. A bulletin board operator can clearly inform the user about the type of material a site or message contains and can take steps to verify and control who is reading or downloading information by restricting access or other privileges to individual computer addresses, to geographic areas or institutions, or to subscribers who have provided some evidence (for example, credit card number or copy of driver's license) of age or identity.

Most Internet users and service providers already take steps to "channel" indecent material away from children — motivated by common sense and professional judgment, rather than by legal compulsion. For example, virtually all "adult" Internet sites contain bold warning screens through which users pass before accessing sexually explicit material. Some sites require confirmation that the user is age 18 or 21 or older, and that he or she understands that sexually explicit expression is available on the site. Most newsgroup titles (for example, "alt.sex.stories") clearly indicate the subject matter of the messages posted there. And most e-mail and newsgroup messages contain "headers" — the electronic equivalent to the "Re:" line in paper memos — that tell the reader what to expect. Those headers are displayed before any sexually explicit expression is accessed.

Some providers limit access to sexually explicit expression to users with a password, which is supplied only upon proof, not just affirmation, of age. An increasing number of "adult" sites subscribe to age-verification services, such as Adult Check, Adult Pass, and Validate. For a modest one-time or annual fee, these services verify a user's age and then issue a password that can be used when accessing sexually explicit sites. This is reminiscent of the techniques used by providers of so-called "dial-a-porn" services. In that context, the Supreme Court has held the use of technologically unsophisticated mechanisms, such as requiring use of a credit card, to be legally sufficient to distinguish between adult and minor customers.[14] As the Internet becomes more commercial and the primary source of sexually explicit information shifts from noncommercial to commercial providers, the number of Internet sites requiring passwords, subscriptions, or payment to access cybersex is growing.

These traits of the Internet medium and the behavior of most information providers led the Supreme Court to conclude:

> Though such material is widely available, users seldom encounter such content accidentally. "A document's title or a description of the document will usually appear before the document itself. . . and in many cases the user will receive detailed information about a site's content before he or she need take the step to access the document. Almost all sexually explicit images are preceded by warnings as to the content." For that reason, the "odds are slim" that a user would enter a sexually explicit site by accident. Unlike communications received by radio or television, "the receipt of information on the Internet requires a series of affirmative steps more deliberate and directed than merely turning a dial. A

child requires some sophistication and some ability to read to retrieve material and thereby to use the Internet unattended."[15]

The Internet also facilitates the use of technologies to regulate access to specified content. The district court in *American Civil Liberties Union* v. *Reno* identified a variety of existing and emerging products — which now include Cyber Snoop, CyberPatrol, CYBERsitter, Internet Filter, NetNanny, Net-Rated, Net Snitch, SafeSearch, SmartFilter, SurfWatch, WebTrack, and X-Stop, among others — for controlling access by minors and found that the "market for this type of software is growing, and there is increasing competition among software providers to provide products."[16]

These software filters are evolving quite rapidly, but generally they offer three types of services: site blocking, content blocking, and session recording. Site blocking is the most basic and widespread feature of software filters. Once installed, the software refers to an online list of sites and blocks access to those sites, unless a password is entered. The lists are developed by panels of reviewers, which often include parents and teachers, and include web sites and newsgroups that are known to feature sexually explicit information. More recent versions of these site-blocking packages permit a very high degree of customization, based on user, time of day, and type of information to be blocked. For example, CyberPatrol, one of the most popular filtering packages, enables parents to selectively block access to any or all of 12 categories of Internet content:

- Violence/Profanity: Extreme cruelty, physical or emotional acts against any animal or person that are intended primarily to hurt or inflict pain. Obscene words, phrases, and profanity defined as text that uses George Carlin's seven censored words more often than once every 50 messages or pages.
- Partial Nudity: Full or partial exposure of the human anatomy except when exposing genitalia.
- Nudity: Any exposure of the human genitalia.
- Sexual Acts (graphic or text): Pictures or text exposing anyone or anything involved in explicit sexual acts and lewd and

73

lascivious behavior, including masturbation, copulation, pedophilia, and intimacy and involving nude or partially nude people in heterosexual, bisexual, lesbian, or homosexual encounters. Also includes phone sex ads, dating services, adult personals, CD-ROMs, and videos.

- Gross Depictions (graphic or text): Pictures or descriptive text of anyone or anything that are crudely vulgar, deficient in civility or behavior, or showing scatological impropriety. Includes such depictions as maiming, bloody figures, indecent depiction of bodily functions.

- Racism/Ethnic Impropriety: Prejudice or discrimination against any race or ethnic culture. Ethnic or racist jokes and slurs. Any text that elevates one race over another.

- Satanic/Cult: Worship of the devil; affinity for evil, wickedness. Sects or groups that potentially coerce individuals in order to grow, and keep, their membership.

- Drugs/Drug Culture: Topics dealing with the use of illegal drugs for entertainment. This would exclude current illegal drugs used for medicinal purposes (for example, drugs used to treat victims of AIDS). Includes substances used for other than their primary purpose to alter the individual's state of mind, such as glue sniffing.

- Militant/Extremist: Extremely aggressive and combative behaviors, radicalism, advocacy of extreme political measures. Topics include extreme political groups that advocate violence as a means to achieve their goal.

- Gambling: Relating to lotteries, casinos, betting, numbers games, and online sports or financial betting, and including non-monetary dares.

- Questionable/Illegal: Material or activities of a dubious nature that may be illegal in any or all jurisdictions, such as illegal business schemes, chain letters, software piracy, and copyright infringement.

- Alcohol, Beer, and Wine: Material pertaining to the sale or consumption of alcoholic beverages. Also includes sites and information relating to tobacco products.[17]

The list of sites blocked by each category is updated regularly. For example, SurfWatch offers a new list to subscribers every day; the users' computers are updated automatically when they activate their Internet browser. The SurfWatch list reportedly included more than 40,000 sites as of August 1997. These site-blocking programs work with direct Internet service providers and with commercial online services, such as CompuServe and America Online. In fact, all of the major online services now offer their members access to some form of site-blocking software. The software also can be purchased for about $20, with subscriptions to list updates costing approximately $60 per year.

The second and emerging type of filter software blocks specific content, rather than sites. These programs are very useful for controlling access to e-mail messages, which are not screened by site-blocking software. Content-blocking packages also can be used to restrict the information transmitted from the user's computer, thereby allowing a parent to prevent a child from conducting Internet searches for sexually explicit words or phrases or from giving away his or her name or address. For example, ChatGuard, a companion program to CyberPatrol, allows parents to enter words or character strings on a ChatGuard list. Then, when the child types these words or character strings, the listed words, characters, or phrases are replaced by "xxxx."

The third type of software designed to control minors' access to specific expression imposes no technological barrier to such information; rather, it saves a list of Internet sites visited and the time of day and duration of each visit. The list is stored in an encrypted, password-protected file on the user's computer, so that a parent or teacher can later "audit" the material that the minor has accessed on the Internet. Cyber Snoop and Net Snitch are two widely available examples of this type of program.

In addition to site-blocking, content-blocking, and session-recording software, all of the commercial online service providers offer additional, specialized, parental control options to their members. These providers give their subscribers the option of blocking access to the Internet and allow parents to tailor the services to which their children have access. America Online offers an online area designed specifically for children. The "Kids Only" parental control feature allows parents to establish an America Online account for their children that accesses only the Kids Only channel on America Online.

A new effort by a consortium of major World Wide Web developers and users is developing technical standards that would support parents' and educators' ability to filter and screen material that children see on the Web. PICS — the "Platform for Internet Content Selection" — permits third parties, as well as individual content providers, to rate content on the Internet in a variety of ways. As described by two of the system's principal developers, "PICS provides neither selection software nor a rating system. It simply establishes conventions for describing rating systems and for label formats, so that PICS-compatible software can read labels from any source. It also establishes technical specifications for label distribution, so that software from different vendors can exchange labels."[18] PICS currently is available in Microsoft's Internet Explorer and will be included in Netscape Navigator 5.0.

PICS is a potentially significant tool in setting the technical standards necessary to allow users to use a variety of rating systems when filtering sites. The ultimate goal is that all web browsers will offer users the option of choosing the types of sites to which the software will permit access. A PICS-equipped browser could contain a list of either restricted sites or permitted sites, or it could block access to all sites that have not been rated by a PICS rating service while allowing access to sites that have an acceptable PICS rating. Information providers could rate their own sites, third parties could rate sites, or the user's browser could refer to multiple sources of rating information.

Despite the existence of software filters and online controls and the promise of PICS, technologies are not a panacea for controlling children's access to sexually explicit expression. They all require affirmative steps to acquire and activate. Most of these technologies must be purchased and require some form of ongoing subscription. In addition, the site-blocking programs all rely on ratings conducted by third parties, who may have dramatically different tastes and values than other adult users.

While software can effectively screen for suggestive words or for known sexually explicit sites, it cannot now screen for sexually explicit images if they are not accompanied by suggestive text and do not originate from a listed site. Moreover, the sheer volume of data on the Internet means that there will always be some delay before a site is rated or before a site's rating is updated. And it is impossible to verify the speed and quality of rating services, because the lists are kept secret to prevent them from being used as a guide to "banned" material on the Internet.

Perhaps most important, all of these programs have the effect of screening out information that may be appropriate and desirable for children, especially older children. This is because it is difficult to account for the context in which suspect words are used. For example, SurfWatch originally screened for the word "couples," thereby excluding many inoffensive sites, include the White House web server. SurfWatch also reportedly blocks access to articles and news stories about AIDS, HIV, and homosexuality. NetNanny blocks access to the U.S. Central Intelligence Agency and the National Organization of Women. CyberPatrol, depending on the categories chosen by users, will block sites that frequently use the words "gay," "bisexual," "homosexual," "lesbian," "male," "men," "boy," "activities," or "rights." This not only has the effect of denying children access to important segments of the Internet, it also skews the political and intellectual variety of material to which they have access.

Despite these limitations, filtering software has been widely employed not only by online service providers, but also by companies wishing to control their employees' access to non-work-related sites (businesses now account for 30% of SurfWatch sales), by schools, and by libraries. This last use is particularly controversial, because the American Library Association recently adopted a resolution opposing the use of "filtering software by libraries to block access to constitutionally protected speech" as a violation of the Library Bill of Rights.[19] This resolution is consistent with the ALA's long-standing opposition to any restrictions on the materials that any patron may use. This is clear not only from Article V of the ALA's Bill of Rights — "A person's right to use a library should not be denied or abridged because of origin, age, background, or views"[20] — but also in the ALA's resolutions on Free Access to Libraries for Minors, Access for Children and Young People to Videotapes and Other Nonprint Formats, and Access to Electronic Information, Services, and Networks. All of these documents provide that "the rights of users who are minors shall in no way be abridged"[21] and that "policies which set minimum age limits for access to videotapes and/or audiovisual materials and equipment, with or without parental permission, abridge library use for minors."[22]

This absolutist position is controversial and, in light of state law concerning material that is harmful to minors and community values, arguably difficult to justify. In the case of public school classrooms, which children attend compulsorily, it would be even more difficult to maintain. But it does highlight the vexing issue posed by technological efforts to control access to online content, because those efforts by definition interfere with a minor's quest for knowledge and, inevitably, block access to valuable material.

Ultimately, responsibility for monitoring and controlling access rests with Internet users themselves and, in the case of children, with their parents, teachers, and other adults charged with their supervision. If the child is old enough and skilled enough to seek Internet access to sexually explicit expression, there is little that supervisors can realistically do to prevent that. Inexpensive software exists to record such access, so that it can be detected afterward; but it is impossible to employ technologies to prevent it absolutely. The difficulties surrounding controlling willful children are by no means limited to the Internet. The technologies available to parents and teachers certainly give them more tools to control behavior in the virtual world than are often available in the physical world.

The problem many parents, educators, government regulators, and courts have worried more about is accidental exposure of unsuspecting minors to sexually explicit images. The reasons why that is unlikely have already been outlined and are accepted today by courts. Even in the event of accidental exposure, however, there is reason to believe that online indecency may have less of an effect on children, particularly younger children, than print or broadcast indecency. Internet technologies require the active involvement of the user. Unlike television, content does not pour over the passive receiver who merely turns on the set or, at most, changes the channel. It is not just that Internet content requires affirmative steps to receive, the Internet is a fundamentally interactive environment. The user finds content only if he or she looks, and what the user finds depends largely on how and where he or she looks. Internet content comes in discrete fragments of information — jumbled postings to a list, excerpted paragraphs or sentences, images without explanatory text. Rather than a logical and sequential presentation of information, Internet content often comes in no particular order, "hyperlinked" so that each user may — indeed, must — proceed through the universe of available material in his or her own way.

Television and radio programming are designed to tell a story, to present information in one certain order, to persuade, inform, or entertain. Even the most passive or immature viewer or listener can often understand some part of what is intended to be conveyed. This is what makes television advertising so effective: Images, sound, motion, and text are all combined to sell a product or service. To see what is on next, the viewer cannot effectively avoid the pitch. The Internet could not be more different. What is on next is determined by the user. If the user sits passively, nothing happens; the screen remains blank. This is why Internet advertising is so ineffective; it is so easy to interrupt, stop, or avoid altogether.

The Internet may present less risk than does broadcasting or print that children will be exposed to sexually explicit material. And if there is exposure, there may be less risk of harm. However, while there is little legal compulsion on schools and libraries to control children's access to Internet content, there nevertheless are legitimate reasons why it might be thought desirable to do so.

Notes

1. Federal law today prohibits the sale of "an obscene visual depiction" on federal property; the mailing, importation, and interstate transportation of obscene matter; selling obscene material that has been "shipped or transported in interstate or foreign commerce"; the distribution of obscene matter by cable television; the transmission of obscenity by telephone in the District of Columbia or across state lines; and the broadcasting of obscene language "by means of radio communication." 18 U.S.C. §§ 1460-69, 47 U.S.C. § 223 (1988 & Supp. 1993).
2. United States v. Thomas, CR-94-20019-G (W.D. Tenn. 28 July 1994) (verdict).
3. United States v. Thomas, CR-94-20019-G (W.D. Tenn. 13 December 1994) (conviction and forfeiture order), *aff'd,* 74 F.3d 701 (6th Cir. 1996).
4. Brief for amicus curiae Electronic Frontier Foundation, p. 4, Thomas v. United States, Nos. 94-6648 and 94-6649 (6th Cir.).
5. 413 U.S. 20.
6. United States v. Thomas, 74 F.3d 701 (6th Cir. 1996).
7. American Civil Liberties Union v. Reno, 929 F. Supp. 824, 843 (E.D. Pa. 1996), *aff'd,* _ U.S. _, 1997 U.S. LEXIS 4037 (1997).
8. Id., p. 849.
9. Burns Indiana Code Annotated § 35-49-2-2 (1996).
10. Id. § 35-49-3-3.
11. Id. § 35-49-3-4.
12. Federal Communications Commission v. Pacifica Foundation, 438 U.S. 726, 749 (1978).
13. Cruz v. Ferre, 755 F.2d 1415, 1419-22 (11th Cir. 1985); Community Television of Utah, Inc. v. Wilkinson, 611 F. Supp. 1099, 1113 (D. Utah 1985), *aff'd,* 800 F.2d 989 (10th Cir. 1986), *aff'd,* 480 U.S. 926 (1987).
14. Carlin Communications, Inc. v. Federal Communications Commission, 837 F.2d 546 (2d Cir.), *cert. denied,* 488 U.S. 928 (1988).
15. _ U.S. at _, 1997, U.S. LEXIS 4037, p. *20 (quoting American Civil Liberties Union v. Reno, 929 F. Supp. 824) (footnotes omitted).
16. 929 F. Supp. p. 839.
17. Id., p. 840.
18. Paul Resnick and James Miller, *PICS: Internet Access Controls*

Without Censorship (available at http://www.bilkent.edu.tr/pub/ WWW/PICS/iacwc.htm).

19. *Resolution on the Use of Filtering Software in Libraries*, adopted by the American Library Association Council, 2 July 1997.

20. *Library Bill of Rights,* adopted by the American Library Association Council, 18 June 1948, amended 2 February 1961, and 23 January 1980.

21. *Free Access to Libraries for Minors,* adopted by the American Library Association Council, 30 June 1972, amended 1 July 1981 and 3 July 1991.

22. *Access for Children and Young People to Videotapes and Other Nonprint Formats,* adopted by the American Library Association Council, 28 June 1989.

CHAPTER FIVE

THE VALUE OF INTERNET EXPRESSION

Legislatures and courts have largely assumed, with surprisingly little discussion, that access to sexually explicit expression is harmful to minors. While that conclusion has intuitive appeal, it is beyond the topic of this book to attempt to either support or refute it. Instead, in this final chapter I identify some of the key reasons why lawmakers might nonetheless hesitate before attempting to restrict sexually explicit expression on the Internet, whether for adults or children.

Adults and Expression on the Internet

The Internet may prove to be a particularly appropriate medium for sexually explicit expression. Not only do its technological, structural, and economic features facilitate society's interest in protecting children and preventing other negative side-effects of sexually explicit expression. Those same features also make the Internet a powerful and practical medium for serving society's interest in free expression.

According to the marketplace metaphor for the First Amendment, "[d]iscussion must be kept open no matter how certainly true an accepted opinion may seem to be; many of the most widely acknowledged truths have turned out to be erroneous."[1] It is therefore important that all expression — whether viewed as true or false, mainstream or outrageous — be placed before the public and that the public have a meaningful opportunity to receive whatever ideas that expression may convey. In short, it is in the marketplace that ideas are tested. If society values the marketplace as a means of evaluating ideas, then it is important that ideas about sexuality, some of which may border on the obscene, be included. Otherwise, their value is never tested.

The marketplace metaphor also recognizes that the government may not restrict expression merely because it disagrees with it. Whether or not an idea is lost as a result of the government's regulation of sexually explicit expression on the Internet, it is anathema in a democratic society for the government to regulate expression according to taste. "The fact that society may find speech offensive is not a sufficient reason for suppressing it," the Supreme Court wrote in 1989. "Indeed, if it is the speaker's opinion that gives offense, that consequence is a reason for according it constitutional protection. For it is a central tenet of the First Amendment that the government must remain neutral in the marketplace of ideas."[2] Instead of regulation, the preferred "remedy" for dangerous expression is more, healthier expression. Justice Brandeis wrote in 1927 that "the fitting remedy for evil counsels is good ones. Believing in the power of reason as applied through public discussion, they [the Framers] eschewed silence coerced by law — the argument of force in its worst form."[3]

The value of free expression is experienced not only by the originator of the expression, but by society as a whole, particularly if the opportunity for expression ameliorates the likelihood of acting on antisocial ideas. Moreover, the expression of antisocial ideas elicits expressive responses to those ideas. By limiting the ability of individuals to express publicly their own sexual mores and by restricting opportunities for people to identify adults with similar sexual mores, laws curbing free expression on the Internet may encourage discontent and violence and may deny society the opportunity to prevent violence. Suppressing expression may give the illusion that the ideas that otherwise would have been expressed no longer exist, but it does not lead to the eradication of practices, sexual or otherwise, to which parts of the society may object.

The importance of expression in the marketplace and to individuals certainly does not mean that all expression must be permitted. The solicitation of minors or the depiction of minors in sexual acts should be and is prohibited, because in those situations courts have found that the harm to the individual minors involved outweighs society's or any individual's interest in expression. However, the importance of expression does suggest that child pornography should not, at least under current judicial reasoning, be subject to special restraint if it does not involve real minors. Digital technology makes it possible to produce "childless" child pornography on the Internet. The use of digital technologies to fabricate, rather than photograph, children engaged in sexual acts may result in more children being spared inappropriate and illegal sexual contact.[4]

The Internet is a particularly important medium for diverse expression because of its accessibility to adults. It gives a voice and the opportunity to access a larger audience to people who otherwise would effectively have neither. Any person with a computer and a telephone line can become an author, an artist, a creator. Digital technologies facilitate creativity in text, graphics, and sound. Moreover, digital technologies are comparatively affordable. While it takes millions of dollars to operate a television station or publish a newspaper — the only way of guaranteeing the opportunity to broadcast or publish ideas — it takes only a few dollars a month to broadcast or publish on the Internet to a potential audience that may exceed that of the country's largest television station or newspaper.

The Internet is open, in a way that television and newspapers are not. It is also egalitarian: The real test of expression and ideas is their own value, not the status or affiliation of their source. As Justice Holmes wrote in *Abrams* v. *United States*, "the best test of truth is the power of thought to get itself accepted in the competition of the market."[5] The Internet provides physical safety, convenience, and the anonymity and privacy that facilitate genuine self-expression, even of antisocial thoughts. Moreover, if the expression is objectionable, it is easy for adult users to avoid, because of headers and other indicators of content; to dismiss with the delete key; or to respond. It is difficult to imagine a medium that better serves American values concerning expression.

The accessibility, security, and anonymity of the Internet for adults, combined with the ability to restrict access to inappropriate material by children, make it an ideal medium for serving the values the Supreme Court identified in *Stanley* v. *Georgia* — the fundamental "right to receive information and ideas, regardless of their social worth" and the "right to be free, except in very limited circumstances, from unwanted governmental intrusion into one's privacy."[6] If "our whole constitutional heritage rebels at the thought of giving government the power to control men's minds,"[7] as Justice Marshall wrote for the Court in *Stanley*, then technology may eliminate the need to permit the government that power.

The Value of Unrestrained Expression for Children

Efforts to restrict minors' access to divergent expression also threaten important values for children. The Supreme Court has repeatedly recognized that content-based regulation of expression inevitably leads to restrictions on otherwise inoffensive speech as a result of the difficulty of differentiating between types of speech and because of the natural tendency to self-censor when near the border of suspect expression. For example, although the Supreme Court has repeatedly acknowledged that there is "no constitutional value in false statements of fact,"[8] the Court regularly interprets the First Amendment to protect such statements. The justification for this apparent conflict is that a rule of strict liability separating "true" expression from "false," or protected from unprotected, would necessarily deter some "true" or protected expression, either because of errors by judges or because of "self-censorship" by publishers in an effort to avoid liability. To avoid penalizing "true" or protected expression, the Court often carves out an area of "breathing space" around expression that it believes warrants protection under the First Amendment. "Although the erroneous statement of fact is not worthy of constitutional protection," Justice Powell wrote for the Court in 1974, "[t]he First Amendment requires that we protect some falsehood in order to protect speech that matters."[9]

But efforts to regulate minors' access to sexually explicit expression threaten more than just non-sexually explicit expression that is inadvertently, but inevitably, also affected. Children may have a legitimate interest in accessing some or all of the material that adults would target for restriction. For example, restricting minors' access to the "alt.sex" newsgroups would necessarily block access to "alt.sex.safe" and "alt.sex.abstinence." The information in these newsgroups, while sexually explicit, might nonetheless be of value to junior and senior high school students. As the U.S. District Court for the Eastern District of Pennsylvania noted in *American Civil Liberties Union* v. *Reno*, "one quarter of all new HIV infections in the United States is estimated to occur in young people between the ages of 13 and 20. . . . [G]raphic material . . . post[ed] on the Internet could help save lives."[10] We can regret that teenagers are sexually active and that AIDS will threaten so many of their lives, but denying them meaningful access to information about sexual activities and safe sex practices will not make those statistics go away. The absence of information will only exacerbate the problem.

Minors may have a legitimate interest in sexually explicit expression, even if based solely on curiosity and the role that such information plays in their own development and maturing — what the Supreme Court has characterized as the student's right "to inquire, to study and to evaluate, to gain new maturity and understanding."[11] The Court has long recognized that students do not "shed their constitutional rights to freedom of speech or expression at the schoolhouse gate."[12] One of the earliest statements of this principle came in 1943 when, at the height of World War II, the Supreme Court struck down a state board of education resolution that compelled students to salute the flag while reciting a specific pledge of allegiance.[13] In one of the Court's most eloquent

opinions on the purpose and power of the First Amendment —
even when applied to children in school — Justice Jackson wrote,
"If there is any fixed star in our constitutional constellation, it is
that no official, high or petty, can prescribe what shall be orthodox
in politics, nationalism, religion, or other matters of opinion, or
force citizens to confess by word or act their faith therein."[14] For
government officials to attempt to do so "transcends constitutional limitations on their power and invades the sphere of intellect
and spirit which it is the purpose of the First Amendment to our
Constitution to reserve from all official control."[15] The fact that
children and a public school setting are involved only heightens
the need for "scrupulous protection of Constitutional freedoms of
the individual, if we are not to strangle the free mind at its source
and teach youth to discount important principles of our government as mere platitudes."[16]

Twenty-six years later, at the height of the Vietnam war, the Supreme Court considered how far students' First Amendment rights
extend in *Tinker* v. *Des Moines Independent Community School
District*.[17] Striking down the suspensions of Mary Beth Tinker,
John Tinker, and Christopher Eckhardt for wearing black arm-
bands in protest of the war, the Court stressed in an opinion by
Justice Fortas:

> "[I]n our system, undifferentiated fear or apprehension of
> disturbance is not enough to overcome the right to freedom of
> expression. Any departure from absolute regimentation may
> cause trouble. Any variation from the majority's opinion may
> inspire fear. Any word spoken, in class, in the lunchroom, or
> on the campus, that deviates from the views of another person
> may start an argument or cause a disturbance. But our
> Constitution says we must take this risk, and our history says
> that it is this sort of hazardous freedom — this kind of open-
> ness — that is the basis of our national strength and of the
> independence and vigor of Americans who grow up and live
> in this relatively permissive, often disputatious, society.[18]

Justice Fortas concluded: "In our system, students may not be
regarded as closed-circuit recipients of only that which the State
chooses to communicate."[19]

In 1982, in *Board of Education* v. *Pico*,[20] the Court considered the power of a public school board to remove specified material from a school library — the situation perhaps most closely analogous to restricting access to material on the Internet. The case involved a challenge by students to a school board order removing certain books from junior and senior high school libraries. The board had characterized the targeted books, which included works by Kurt Vonnegut Jr., Richard Wright, Alice Childress, and Eldridge Cleaver, among other authors, as "anti-American, anti-Christian, anti-[Semitic], and just plain filthy."[21] The students alleged that the board's action violated their First Amendment rights. While noting the existence of limits on students' First Amendment rights, the Court nevertheless distinguished restrictions on expression in the classroom, where attendance and curriculum are compulsory, and as part of school-sponsored activities, which might be perceived as being endorsed by the school, from independent exploration by students in the school library. Justice Brennan's language in the plurality opinion seems well suited to the Internet as well:

> A school library, no less than any other public library, is "a place dedicated to quiet, to knowledge, and to beauty." *Keyishian* v. *Board of Regents* observed that "students must always remain free to inquire, to study and to evaluate, to gain new maturity and understanding." The school library is the principal locus of such freedom. As one District Court has well put it, in the school library "a student can literally explore the unknown, and discover areas of interest and thought not covered by the prescribed curriculum. . . . Th[e] student learns that a library is a place to test or expand upon ideas presented to him, in or out of the classroom."
>
> Petitioners emphasize the inculcative function of secondary education, and argue that they must be allowed unfettered discretion to "transmit community values" through the Island Trees schools. But that sweeping claim overlooks the unique role of the school library. . . . [which] afford[s] them [students] an opportunity at self-education and individual enrichment that is wholly optional. Petitioners might well

defend their claim of absolute discretion in matters of curriculum by reliance upon their duty to inculcate community values. But we think that petitioners' reliance upon that duty is misplaced where, as here, they attempt to extend their claim of absolute discretion beyond the compulsory environment of the classroom, into the school library and the regime of voluntary inquiry that there holds sway.[22]

Justice Brennan then drew on a variety of Supreme Court precedents involving adults to find that the First Amendment not only protected students' freedom of thought and expression, but also their right to receive information.

[W]e think that the First Amendment rights of students may be directly and sharply implicated by the removal of books from the shelves of a school library. Our precedents have focused "not only on the role of the First Amendment in fostering individual self-expression but also on its role in affording the public access to discussion, debate, and the dissemination of information and ideas." And we have recognized that "the State may not, consistently with the spirit of the First Amendment, contract the spectrum of available knowledge." In keeping with this principle, we have held that in a variety of contexts "the Constitution protects the right to receive information and ideas." This right is an inherent corollary of the rights of free speech and press that are explicitly guaranteed by the Constitution, in two senses. First, the right to receive ideas follows ineluctably from the sender's First Amendment right to send them: "The right of freedom of speech and press . . . embraces the right to distribute literature, and necessarily protects the right to receive it." "The dissemination of ideas can accomplish nothing if otherwise willing addressees are not free to receive and consider them. It would be a barren marketplace of ideas that had only sellers and no buyers."

More importantly, the right to receive ideas is a necessary predicate to the recipient's meaningful exercise of his own rights of speech, press, and political freedom.[23]

90

Justice Brennan concluded:

> In sum, just as access to ideas makes it possible for citizens generally to exercise their rights of free speech and press in a meaningful manner, such access prepares students for active and effective participation in the pluralistic, often contentious society in which they will soon be adult members. Of course all First Amendment rights accorded to students must be construed "in light of the special characteristics of the school environment." But the special characteristics of the school library make that environment especially appropriate for the recognition of the First Amendment rights of students.[24]

Recognizing the First Amendment rights, however limited, of students is of limited *legal* significance to a discussion over access by minors to online content, because it is far from clear that those rights in any way obligate public schools and libraries to provide Internet access. And such rights are legally irrelevant in the context of private schools and libraries, because constitutional rights apply only against the government. But the Supreme Court's recognition of students' First Amendment rights is significant because of the logic that undergirds that recognition. Lawmakers and educators should resist limiting the material that students are permitted but not required to access because the information accessed may be valuable in itself, because such access is necessary to individual thought and expression, because disparate information is often challenging and thought-provoking, because the process of sorting through such information is excellent training for broader participation in society, and because imposing limits undermines the toleration and respect — for other people, other ideas, and for the Constitution — that we claim to value. Moreover, efforts to restrict access by minors to sexually explicit expression by imposing liability on the providers of that information inevitably run the risk of driving those information providers from the marketplace. The result is that both adults and older children, for whom such information may be appropriate, are denied all possibility of access.

This does not necessarily lead to the conclusion that there should be no limits on the information available to children. Certainly, depending on the age of students and their level of development, as well as the setting and the nature of the material, some expression may indeed be inappropriate. However, the Court's logic argues for hesitation before using technological or other means for restricting children's access to Internet content, and for sensitivity if it is ultimately thought necessary to do so.

Although beyond the topic of this book, there often are alternatives that are far more desirable — and effective — than absolutely blocking access to specific categories of expression. As a practical matter, younger children probably should not be given access to the Internet at all. CD-ROMs and other software packages offer wonderful learning opportunities for pre-school and younger elementary school children. On the whole, the Internet does not. Once a parent determines that access is appropriate, it is very important, and often overlooked, that children receive training before being given access to the Internet and that they receive adult oversight when using the Internet. Most parents would not send their young children across town on their own; the Internet poses just as many dangers and opportunities. That training should certainly include information on the dangers of the virtual world, just as we regrettably have to warn children about the dangers of the physical world. Children and adults alike need to overcome the complacency and false sense of security that comes from accessing such a technologically neat, inviting medium from the comfort of our homes or schools or libraries. Young Internet users also should be given information on interesting and appropriate sites. Many organizations are providing "kid-friendly" sites and entry points on the Internet; these are a far better starting point for children than the "search" key. In addition, parents, teachers, librarians, and volunteers should browse the Internet with younger children and let older children know that there are adults who care about, and who are available to discuss, what they are finding on the Internet.

The Internet, if thoughtfully integrated into schools and libraries, actually creates important opportunities for teaching children to deal with society more broadly. There is little that is accessible online that cannot be encountered at some point in everyday life. The Internet is a comparatively safe environment for helping minors prepare to deal with those issues, whether it is contact with a stranger, sorting through a flood of information, judging the quality of ideas, or learning to avoid expression that may be harmful.

For older and more mature students, legal and technological restrictions on access to Internet content become less desirable. With fewer restrictions on that access, the opportunities increase for individual exploration, substantive teaching, and demonstrating the constitutional value of free inquiry, thought, and expression. Expanded access and opportunities alter, but do not diminish, the role of responsible adults. Rather than control, parents and teachers might profit most by helping an adolescent process and place in context the material he or she encounters in cyberspace. Some discoveries may require explanation; a few, refutation; and a potentially large number, the opportunity for the adolescent to discuss and analyze in the company of fellow students and adults.

Despite the government's enthusiasm for ensuring universal access to the Internet, cyberspace is no panacea for primary and secondary education. It presents an extraordinary diversity of material from around the world, some of which is clearly inappropriate, particularly for younger children. Fortunately, the Internet offers many technological means for dealing with specific types of online material, such as sexually explicit expression. These technologies are by no means perfect, and they raise additional issues of their own, not the least of which is the financial and personnel cost of installing and updating them. Nevertheless, they provide an increasingly dependable means of protecting younger children from exposure to inappropriate material.

What technologies do not address, and where serious evaluation by educators is most needed, is the wide variety of other significant issues that the Internet poses. For example, even adults have been slow to realize that much of the information available on the Internet is inaccurate, misleading, outdated, or even fraudulent. Because of its lack of hierarchy and low cost of access, Internet users must exercise greater skills of selection and discernment than might be necessary in the case of reading a newspaper or watching television news.

The debate over the Internet already has had the tendency to misfocus national attention and investment in education. In one recent survey, 44% of urban teachers reported that students lacked textbooks to take home; 25% of teachers are using textbooks more than 10 years old; and 76% report paying for books out of their own pockets. In the face of these and similar statistics, the government's push to wire every classroom and library in the country by the year 2000 has led many educators to be dubious about the value of this technological initiative. A recent article in the *Boston Globe,* "Never Mind the Internet, Bill — Give Us Some Textbooks," is typical of the growing cynicism among educators, parents, and journalists about the relative benefit of extending the Internet into crumbling, ill-equipped, understaffed classrooms.[25] Roger Harris, principal of the Timilty Middle School in Roxbury, has mused that government's Internet push is "like being shown the highway but you don't have a vehicle."[26]

The Internet is a tool, a valuable resource. But far from satisfying demand for lower-cost teaching materials, safer classrooms, smaller class sizes, and better qualified teachers and librarians, the Internet exacerbates the need for all of these. As one-time champions of the "paperless society" have learned, once computers enter a school or office, paper use increases. Similarly, computers require space, security, technical support, peripheral equipment (for example, printers, cables, etc.), software, supplies, maintenance, and upgrades. Most important, the successful deployment of the Internet in schools requires training of educators and students and requires the time and resources to thoughtfully integrate the technology into the curriculum. At present, the push for the Internet seems more likely to add to the burdens of already overworked teachers and to expand, not narrow, the gap between well-funded and under-funded schools.

There are many excellent examples in schools and libraries today of appropriate, effective uses of the Internet to educate students. The field is developing very rapidly, with new educational services and sites appearing each day. The legal issues seem at least temporarily put to rest, following the Supreme Court's repudiation of the Communications Decency Act. While the problems of funding, training, and the skillful integration of the Internet in American schools and libraries demand our urgent attention, the extraordinary protection accorded by the First Amendment affords considerable room for educators to address those issues and to experiment with using the Internet in classrooms and libraries.

Notes

1. Thomas Emerson, *The System of Freedom of Expression* (New York: Random House, 1970), pp. 6-7.
2. Federal Communications Commission v. Pacifica Foundation, 438 U.S. 726, 745-56 (1976).
3. Whitney v. California, 274 U.S. 357, 375-76 (1927) (Brandeis, J., concurring).
4. Such expression should be distinguished from that involved in the FBI's recently concluded two-year "Innocent Images" investigation. The operation, which reportedly grew out of a complaint of an America Online customer who received an unsolicited mail message contained an image file depicting two boys engaged in sexual acts, resulted in searches of 125 homes around the country and 12 arrests. According to press reports, the investigation targeted both the transmission of child pornography and the use of computer networks to solicit minors for sexual acts.
5. 250 U.S. 616, 630 (1919) (Holmes, J., dissenting).
6. 394 U.S. 557, 564 (1969).
7. Id., p. 565.
8. Gertz v. Robert Welch, Inc., 418 U.S. 323, 340 (1974).
9. Id., p. 341.
10. American Civil Liberties Union v. Reno, 929 F. Supp. 824, 853 (E.D. Pa. 1996) (Sloviter, C.J., concurring), *aff'd,* _ U.S. _, 1997 U.S. LEXIS 4037 (1997).
11. Keyishian v. Board of Regents, 385 U.S. 589, 603 (1967).
12. Tinker v. Des Moines Independent Community School District, 393 U.S. 503, 506 (1969).
13. West Virginia State Board of Education v. Barnette, 319 U.S. 624 (1943).

14. Id., p. 642.
15. Id.
16. Id., p. 637.
17. 393 U.S. 503 (1969).
18. 393 U.S. at 508-509 (citation omitted).
19. Id., p. 511.
20. 457 U.S. 853 (1982).
21. Id., p. 857.
22. Id. at 868-69 [quoting Brown v. Louisiana, 383 U.S. 131, 142 (1966); *Keyishian,* 385 U.S. at 603; Right to Read Defense Committee v. School Committee, 454 F. Supp. 703, 715 (Mass. 1978)] (citations and footnote omitted).
23. Id., pp. 866-67 [quoting First National Bank of Boston v. Bellotti, 435 U.S. 765, 783 (1978); Griswold v. Connecticut, 381 U.S. 479, 482 (1965); Stanley v. Georgia, 394 U.S. 557, 564 (1969); Martin v. Struthers, 319 U.S. 141, 143 (1943); Lamont v. Postmaster General, 381 U.S. 301, 308 (1965) (Brennan, J., concurring)] (citations omitted).
24. Id., p. 868 (quoting *Tinker*, 393 U.S. at 506) (citation omitted).
25. Derrick Z. Jackson, "Never Mind the Internet, Bill — Give Us Some Textbooks," *Boston Globe*, 14 February 1997, p. A23.
26. Id.

SOURCES FOR FURTHER RESEARCH

Cases

American Civil Liberties Union v. Reno, 929 F. Supp. 824 (E.D. Pa. 1996), aff'd, _ U.S. _, 1997 U.S. LEXIS 4037 (1997).

Board of Education v. Pico, 457 U.S. 853 (1982).

Cohen v. California, 403 U.S. 15 (1971).

Federal Communications Commission v. Pacifica Foundation, 438 U.S. 726 (1978).

Miller v. California, 413 U.S. 15 (1973).

Reno v. American Civil Liberties Union, _ U.S. _, 1997 U.S. LEXIS 4037 (1997).

Sable Communications of California, Inc. v. Federal Communications Commission, 492 U.S. 115 (1989).

Stanley v. Georgia, 394 U.S. 557 (1969).

Texas v. Johnson, 491 U.S. 397 (1989).

Tinker v. Des Moines Independent Community School District, 393 U.S. 503 (1969).

West Virginia State Board of Education v. Barnette, 319 U.S. 624 (1943).

Secondary Materials

Bass, Timothy S.T. "Obscenity in Cyberspace: Some Reasons for Retaining the Local Community Standard." *1996 University of Chicago Legal Forum*, p. 471.

"Beyond the Internet: Settling the Electronic Frontier," *Stanford Law & Policy Review* 6 (1994) (entire issue).

Burke, Debra D. "Cybersmut and the First Amendment: A Call for a New Obscenity Standard." *Harvard Journal of Law and Technology* 9 (1996): 87.

Cannon, Robert. "The Legislative History of Senator Exon's Communications Decency Act: Regulating Barbarians on the Information Superhighway." *Federal Communications Law Journal* 49 (1996): 51.

Cate, Fred H. *Privacy in the Information Age*. Washington, D.C.: Brookings Institution Press, 1997.

Cate, Fred H. "The Technological Transformation of Copyright Law." *Iowa Law Review* 81 (1996): 1395.

Cate, Fred H. "Cybersex: Regulating Sexually Explicit Expression on the Internet." *Behavioral Sciences & the Law* 14 (1996): 145.

Cate, Fred H. "The First Amendment and the National Information Infrastructure." *Wake Forest Law Review* 30 (1995): 1.

Cate, Fred H. "Indecency, Intolerance, and Ignorance: The First Amendment and the Regulation of Electronic Expression." *Journal of On-Line Law* (1995): 5.

Cate, Fred H. "A Law Antecedent and Paramount." *Federal Communications Law Journal* 47 (1994): 205.

Cate, Fred H. "The National Information Infrastructure: Policymakers and Policymaking." *Stanford Law & Policy Review* 6 (1994): 43.

Chiu, Dennis W. "Obscenity on the Internet: Local Community Standards for Obscenity Are Unworkable on the Information Superhighway." *Santa Clara Law Review* 36 (1995): 185.

Clapes, Anthony L. "The Wages of Sin: Pornography and Internet Providers." *Computer Lawyer* 13 (July 1996): 1.

"Computer Legislation." *Harvard Journal on Legislation* 34 (1997) (entire issue).

Corn-Revere, Robert. "New Age Comstockery." *CommLaw Conspectus* 4 (1996): 173.

Dupre, Anne Proffitt. "Should Students Have Constitutional Rights? Keeping Order in the Public Schools." *George Washington Law Review* 65 (1996): 49.

Ennis, Bruce J. "Applying the First Amendment in the Information Age." *Patents, Copyrights, Trademarks, and Literary Property Course Handbook Series*, Practicing Law Institute (November 1996): 881.

Exon, Senator Jim. "The Communications Decency Act." *Federal Communications Law Journal* 49 (1996): 95.

Faucette, Jeffrey E. "The Freedom of Speech at Risk in Cyberspace: Obscenity Doctrine and a Frightened University's Censorship of Sex on the Internet." *Duke Law Journal* 44 (1995): 1155.

Friedman, Meredith Leigh. "Keeping Sex Safe on the Information Superhighway: Computer Pornography and the First Amendment." *New York Law School Law Review* 40 (1996): 1025.

Goldman, Robert F. "Put Another Log on the Fire, There's a Chill on the Internet: The Effect of Applying Current Anti-Obscenity Laws to Online Communications." *Georgia Law Review Association* 29 (1995): 1075.

Hardy, Trotter. "Law and the Internet: What Are the Dangers of Putting the World at Your Fingertips?" *Business Law Today* 5 (1996): 8.

Hefner, Marion D. " 'Roast Pigs' and Miller-Light: Variable Obscenity in the Nineties." *University of Illinois Law Review* (1996): 843.

Heumann, Douglas C. "United States v. Thomas: Will the Community Standard Be Roadkill on the Information Superhighway?" *Western State University Law Review* 23 (1995): 189.

Johns, Michael. "The First Amendment and Cyberspace: Trying to Teach Old Doctrines New Tricks." *University of Cincinnati Law Review* 46 (1996): 1383.

Johnson, Dawn L. "It's 1996: Do You Know Where Your Cyberkids Are? Captive Audiences and Content Regulation on the Internet." *John Marshall Journal of Computer and Information Law* 15 (1996): 51.

Johnson, Peter. "Pornography Drives Technology: Why Not to Censor the Internet." *Federal Communications Law Journal* 49 (1996): 217.

Keane, William P. "Impact of the Communications Decency Act of 1996 on Federal Prosecutions of Computer Dissemination of Obscenity, Indecency, and Child Pornography." *Hastings Communications and Entertainment Law Journal (Comm/Ent)* 18 (1996): 853.

Kushner, David. "The Communications Decency Act and the Indecent Indecency Spectacle." *Hastings Communications and Entertainment Law Journal (Comm/Ent)* 19 (1996): 87.

Lim, Frederick B. "Obscenity and Cyberspace: Community Standards in an On-Line World." *Columbia-VLA Journal of Law and the Arts* 20 (1996): 291.

"Marketing Pornography on the Information Superhighway." *Georgetown Law Journal* 83 (1995) (entire issue).

McKay, Laura J. "The Communications Decency Act: Protecting Children from On-Line Indecency." *Seton Hall Legislation Journal* 20 (1996): 463.

Metcalf, Todd. "Obscenity Prosecutions in Cyberspace: The Miller Test Cannot Go Where No [Porn] Has Gone Before." *Washington University Law Quarterly* 74 (1996): 481.

Peters, Robert W. "There Is a Need to Regulate Indecency on the Internet." *Cornell Journal of Law and Public Policy* 6 (1977): 363.

Petrie, Sean J. "Indecent Proposals: How Each Branch of the Federal Government Overstepped Its Institutional Authority in the Development of Internet Obscenity Law." *Stanford Law Review* 49 (1997): 637.

Rappaport, Stacey J. "Rules of the Road: The Constitutional Limits of Restricting Indecent Speech on the Information Superhighway." *Fordham Intellectual Property, Media & Entertainment Law Journal* 6 (1995): 301.

Rivera-Sanchez, Milagros. "How Far Is Too Far? The Line Between 'Offensive' and 'Indecent' Speech." *Federal Communications Law Journal* 49 (1997): 327.

Roe, Richard L. "Valuing Student Speech: The Work of the Schools as Conceptual Development." *California Law Review* 79 (1991): 1271.

Saffer, Ian L. "Obscenity Law and the Equal Protection Clause: May States Exempt Schools, Libraries, and Museums from Obscenity Statutes?" *New York University Law Review* 70 (1995): 397.

Shiff, Sean Adam. "The Good, the Bad and the Ugly: Criminal Liability for Obscene and Indecent Speech on the Internet." *William Mitchell Law Review* 22 (1996): 731.

Smolla, Rodney A. "Freedom of Speech for Libraries and Librarians." *Law Library Journal* 85 (1993): 71

Smolla, Rodney A. *Free Speech in an Open Society*. New York: Alfred A. Knopf, 1992.

"Symposium: Cyberspace and the Law." *St. John's Journal of Legal Commentary* 11 (1996): 617.

"Symposium: The Information Superhighway: A Critical Discussion of its Possibilities and Legal Implications." *Wake Forest Law Review* 30 (1995): 1.

"Symposium: Legal Issues in the Information Revolution." *Houston Law Review* 32 (1995): 303.

"Symposium: Legal Regulation of the Internet." *Connecticut Law Review* 28 (1996): 653.

"Symposium: Pornography: Free Speech or Censorship in Cyberspace?" *Boston University Journal of Science and Technology Law* 3 (1997): 3.

Valente, William D. *Education Law: Public and Private*. St. Paul, Minn.: West, 1985, and Supplement, 1989.

Wilborn, S. Elizabeth. "Teaching the New Three Rs — Repression, Rights, and Respect: A Primer of Student Speech Activities." *Boston College Law Review* 37 (1995): 119.

Online Resources

Organizations

American Association of School Librarians (http://www.ala.org/aasl/index.html)

American Bar Association/Division for Public Education (http://www.abanet.org/publiced/home.html)

American Civil Liberties Union (http://www.aclu.org)

American Federation of Teachers (http://www.aft.org//index.htm)

American Library Association (http://www.ala.org)

Center for Democracy and Technology (http://www.cdt.org)

Electronic Frontier Foundation (http://www.eff.org)

Electronic Privacy Information Center (http://www.epic.org)

National Association of Elementary School Principals (http://www.naesp.org)

National Association of Secondary School Principals (http://www.nassp.org)

National Education Association (http://www.nea.org)

National School Boards Association (http://www.nsba.org)

Phi Delta Kappa International (http://www.pdkintl.org)

PTA (http://www.pta.org)

U.S. Department of Education (http://www.ed.gov)

U.S. Federal Communications Commission/LearnNet (http://www.fcc.gov/learnnet)

U.S. Information Infrastructure Task Force (http://iitf.doc.gov)

U.S. Library of Congress (http://www.loc.gov)

Software Filters

Bess (http://bess.net)

Cyber Snoop (http://www.pearlsw.com)

CyberPatrol (http://www.cyberpatrol.com)

CYBERsitter (http://www.solidoak.com/cysitter.htm)

Internet Filter (http://www.ksc.co.th/filter.html)

NetNanny (http://www.netnanny.com)

Net-Rated (http://www.netrated.com)

Net Shepard (http://www.shepherd.net)

Net Snitch (http://www.netsnitch.com)

PICS (http://www.bilkent.edu.tr/pub/www/pics)

SafeSearch (http://www.safesearch.com)

SmartFilter (http://www.webster.com)

SurfWatch (http://www.surfwatch.com)

WebTrack (http://webtrack.webster.com)

X-Stop (http://www.xstop.com)

ABOUT THE AUTHOR

Fred H. Cate is a professor of law, Louis F. Niezer Faculty Fellow, and director of the Information Law and Commerce Institute at the Indiana University School of Law in Bloomington. An internationally recognized expert on information law, Cate also serves as senior counsel for information law in the Indianapolis law firm of Ice Miller Donadio & Ryan.

Cate is the author of many articles and monographs addressing a wide range of information-related issues, particularly in the context of digital networks. He writes extensively on these topics for professional journals. Cate is the author of *Privacy in the Information Age* and the editor of *Visions of the First Amendment for a New Millennium*. He has served on many government and professional panels and spoken at more than 100 conferences addressing issues in information law. Most recently, he directed the Electronic Information Privacy and Commerce Study for the Brookings Institution. From 1990 until the program's closing in May 1996, he was senior fellow of the Annenberg Washington Program in Communications Policy Studies and served as director of research and projects for that program from 1991 to 1993.

Cate received his J.D. and his A.B. with Honors and Distinction from Stanford University. Before joining the faculty at Indiana University, he practiced in the Washington, D.C., office of Debevoise and Plimpton. Cate is a life member of Phi Beta Kappa Associates and a trustee of National History Day. He is listed in *Who's Who in American Law*.